A Lucky American Ch

SINGULAR LIVES

The Iowa Series in North American Autobiography

Albert E. Stone, Series Editor

American Childhood

BY PAUL ENGLE

FOREWORD BY ALBERT E. STONE

UNIVERSITY OF IOWA PRESS ⰿ IOWA CITY

University of
Iowa Press,
Iowa City 52242
Copyright © 1996
by the University
of Iowa Press

Design by Richard Hendel

"An Old-Fashioned
Christmas" and "Those
Damn Jews" were originally
published in *American
Heritage.* "That Fabulous
Old Fourth of July" and
"Remember Memorial
Day?" were originally
published in *Better Homes
and Gardens.* "Where the
World Seems Right and
Good—The Iowa State
Fair" was originally
published in *Holiday.*

Library of Congress
Cataloging-in-Publication Data
Engle, Paul, 1908–1991
    A lucky American childhood / by Paul
Engle; foreword by Albert E. Stone.
    p.   cm.—(Singular lives)
    ISBN 0-87745-540-6
    1. Engle, Paul, 1908–1991—Childhood
and youth.   2. Cedar Rapids (Iowa)—
Social life and customs.   3. Poets,
American—20th century—Biography.
    I. Title.   II. Series.
PS3509.N44Z468   1996
811 .52—dc20
[B]   95-25871
                                        CIP

ISBN 1-58729-636-5 (pbk)
ISBN 978-1-58729-636-9 (pbk)

Contents

Foreword, *vii*

  by Albert E. Stone

Dedication, *xiii*

Paul Engle: A Poem, *xxi*

Eva, *1*

Tom, *20*

The Drug Scene, *36*

News and the Boy, *54*

The Importance of Uncles, *70*

Hiawatha and My Aunt Bertha, *102*

The Glory of the Senses, *109*

The Horse and I, *135*

Those Damn Jews, *150*

Remember Memorial Day? *162*

That Fabulous Old Fourth of July, *167*

Where the World Seems Right and Good —

  The Iowa State Fair, *173*

Our Dangerous Thanksgiving, *178*

Christmas Eve and My Mother's Hands, *182*

An Old-Fashioned Christmas, *185*

Foreword *By Albert E. Stone*

aul Engle's *A Lucky American Childhood*, the twelfth
volume in Iowa's Singular Lives series, differs from
its predecessors in many respects, most notably in
being unabashedly a paean to childhood and adolescence. There is, in addition, the matter of fame. The young
Paul, though born to a working-class family in a modest neighborhood of Cedar Rapids, Iowa, became the future Paul Engle,
an American poet of international renown, especially in the
thirties (*Worn Earth, American Song, Break the Heart's Anger*)
and forties and fifties (*Poems in Praise* and other collections).
He was as well the famous director of the Writers' Workshop
and the International Writing Program at the University of
Iowa. The list of leading authors who counted him friend and
literary equal is indeed impressive.

Even more than Ray Young Bear and Gary Gildner, poets
and authors of *Black Eagle Child* and *The Warsaw Sparks* in this
series, Paul Engle earned fame by celebrating his midwestern
roots. Iowa now stands in his lyrics as "the great west country
of our destiny." Now in a posthumous memoir he matches in
prose the nostalgic energy that once made him the younger
colleague of Edgar Lee Masters and Carl Sandburg. *A Lucky
American Childhood* is little less than a tour de force of imaginative recall. Readers will savor a succession of vividly recaptured
experiences and emotions of family, city, and countryside.
Engle's is a personal and social history recalling other notable
American autobiographies of boyhood and girlhood, beginning with those of Frederick Douglass, Mark Twain, and John
Muir and coming more recently to the life-stories of, among
others, Russell Baker, Maya Angelou, Frank Conroy, and
Susan Allen Toth.

"I was a universal boy in a universal store," Engle exclaims
of his teenage years as assistant in a Cedar Rapids street-corner
drugstore. An ebullient sense of self—"my ego grew like corn
in August, fast and green"—is tempered by an equal awareness of boyish insecurities and ignorance, both redeemed by

the gift of a memory rooted in an observant, curious, sensuous, outgoing youth. Few autobiographies of boyhood, I would argue (even Mark Twain's), exhibit a keener feel for the sights, smells, and sounds of a child's world. "My nose remembers the complicated smells of our house on that day when a stranger and his wife brought our beaten father home," he writes of his father's bobsled accident: "drugs, Father's barn-smelling clothes, Mother's stew of cabbage, carrot, cheap beef in the kitchen . . . the smell of neat's-foot oil rising through the hot-air ducts. How boring the clean smell of a modern house." No less vividly precise are memories of other, less momentous events. That drugstore, with its naif clerk sitting in a back room, between customers, writing verse, is a shabby, fondly remembered temple of smells—tobacco, cheap perfume, candy, newsprint, syrups and soda fountain flavors, elixirs and other odoriferous medications. Many memoirists will, like Engle, evoke the Thanksgiving and Christmas dinners of the pasts. But many fewer can recapture the complex smells of a horse barn, a Czech butcher shop, a kerosene lamp, or chunks of creosoted telephone poles burning in a poor family's house in a cruel Iowa winter. "How busy our noses were in those years" becomes an apt synecdoche of *A Lucky American Childhood*, one of whose chapters is "The Glory of the Senses."

Though a powerful sense of self sensuously alive from his earliest years permeates this narrative, still Engle's strongest memories and emotions cluster about the portraits of his mother and father. The opening chapters reunite both parents with their small son, whose older brother and two sisters are but shadowy figures. Behind the lovingly detailed descriptions of mother and father looms Engle's wider, more mature concern—to let both parents be themselves while also typifying the gentle and violent impulses in American family and rural life. Though his mother shares with her Reinheimer relatives a gentle acceptance of a life of poverty, grinding work, and a spouse at once brutal and loving, Tom Engle represents even more arrestingly the violent side of the Engle legacy. Hence words like "rage," "furious," "hard," and "loud" echo throughout this story, not only in scenes with Tom Engle but even in neutral artifacts like the family photo Uncle Herm proudly displays of the pelts of wolves he's shot on his Minnesota farm; that snapshot still "howls, cracks, yells" in the author's imagination. Though this violent side of his lineage and life is striking, Engle's deeper allegiance, I think, is to the gentler Reinheimer way of bending and suffering. His mother's silent tears notwithstanding, the story's most touching family moment is the father's death. He suffers his second heart attack while roughly schooling a young horse; his son catches him as he falls from the saddle. It is a scene worthy of a novelist—which Engle has been.

A Lucky American Childhood is indeed a book of sharp emotional and cultural contrasts. Paul Engle himself is a callow youth, shy and sensitive but also self-assertive. The family heritage is one of poverty, hard work, pride, strong feelings masked by rough words. Yet a writer of sensuous power and discrimination emerges convincingly from these tough German American Protestants and the unromantic small-city setting. Engle is apologetic neither about his family's modest status nor the apparent shortcomings of Cedar Rapids as an early-twentieth-century community. The future poet unabashedly recalls sitting once in Mrs. Astor's box at the Met in New York clutching his green stocking cap knitted by the calloused hands of his Iowa mother. When that mother visits her son who's become a Rhodes Scholar at Oxford, her sincere common sense is hailed by the son's English tutor. Another meeting of worlds and times is represented by remembrances of roses. These flowers are first found in the Cedar Rapids garden of an old Englishman, a veteran of the Crimean War. Several of these foreign bushes afford another vision of roses when transplanted to the Engles' humble backyard. Finally, there is the image of lovely roses glimpsed from the window of his Oxford College. A less conventional bridging of Iowa and Europe occurs with the bits of horse manure still clinging to the new Rhodes Scholar's shoes, to the quiet delight of his scout who thinks he knows a horsey gentleman when he smells one's shoes.

Cedar Rapids, in fact, is the site of many of his autobiography's most poignant and powerful chapters. The first recounts Paul's career as newsboy. Few narratives of growing up can top the account of Paul falling into the icy Cedar River, only to be rescued by his fellow newsboys and dried out in the fiery heat of the *Gazette*'s pressroom. Paul pluckily completes his wintry route. But before his steps bring him to his own doorstep he's met many of his regular customers, most notably the last. An epiphany occurs at the last door which Paul opens to deliver the paper (as instructed) to the kitchen. A beautiful, naked woman stands in that warm room, transfixing the newsboy and lingering long in the poet's — and our — imagination.

An even more arresting sequence also opens in Cedar Rapids. The newsboy hears from a prejudiced neighbor that "those damn Jews" have moved in. Baffled ignorance changes as Paul is hired to be the "shabbas goy" who lights Saturday stoves and lamps for several devout Jewish families. Later the fledgling poet is befriended by Gabe, a would-be poet and clothing store owner. When lucky fate transforms the boy into a Rhodes Scholar, Gabe, inspecting his adopted son's shabby clothing, outfits Paul with a suitable wardrobe. This fashionable "Jewish" outfit Engle wears proudly into the aristocratic, anti-Semitic confines of Oxford. By now it is the decade of Hitler. On holiday, the poet travels to Germany to polish the language and savor the poems of Rilke. In Berlin, he's again befriended by an old Jew who gives him a handsome set of Rilke's works in hopes that, on his return to Oxford, Engle will wrangle from the American embassy an exit visa for Rebekah, the dark-eyed daughter. Engle's belated letter to Berlin is returned, marked "Disappeared." "Do not be patient with the frightfulness of the human race. Howl, howl. From your dark cave, howl," he exclaims bitterly. After visiting Auschwitz some years later, he concludes the chapter "Those Damn Jews" with an anguished confession of boyish American ignorance and lingering innocence. "There are nights when I seem to find them staring at me through the window out of that blackness which is no different from that dark world they knew. They accuse me that I did so little for them. I admit my guilt. I can give them nothing but my lifelong love. If I could only touch their hands." Yet within a few years of this tragic brush with Nazi brutality in Berlin, the young Engle published "Atlantic-Passage West," a poetic meditation on his return to America's heartland.

> No, I will not be Virgil, lead you down
> Through the dark underworld and that deep river,
> But Sacajawea, Indian woman of the mountains.

In light of this present, much later memoir, the poet's return to his midwestern prairies is an imaginative announcement that ignores, at least temporarily, some dark complexities and deep rivers. That avoidance, of course, was shared by many Americans in the late thirties. Belatedly but with genuine contrition, the poet accepts and corrects his past in his autobiography. This, after all, is one reason to write one's life history.

Seeing himself from several (sometimes ironic) perspectives is true of *A Lucky American Childhood* almost to the end. If the early chapters celebrate and gently criticize one poet's beginnings within a complex, violent, and loving world, the final chapters—the sequence chronicling the Iowa seasons from Memorial Day to Christmas—frankly traffic in nostalgia, if not sentimentality. On the earlier side of fond consciousness and recall—indeed, at the imaginative center of the story—stands "Those Damn Jews," which dramatizes a plunge into the blacker side of Paul Engle's past. This narrative strategy cannot fail to underscore the stereotypes of the "Iowa State Fair." Readers of *A Lucky American Childhood* will, I predict, find themselves bemused by one side of the immature Iowa self so sensuously and honestly exposed here, yet arrested by a maturer memory alert to darker dimensions in his—and our—world, ones that have emerged since the horse gave way to the automobile.

Dedication

This book is dedicated to my daughters, Mary, Sara, Wei-Wei, and Lan-lan, and to my grandchildren, Mary, Christopher, Sara, Anthea, and Christoph Paul.

> You ask if my old love for you
> Can grow stronger.
> It will through all eternity,
> And light years longer.
> Then longer, longer, longer.

I had a lucky life. Such a way will never be lived here again. It has gone with the wild-buffalo skinners and the Indian fighters, with my mother's hands whose tough calluses tore the sheets as she made my bed, with that marvelous rich reek of harness and saddle leather, of horse manure and sweat, which I happily breathed each day.

Father, working hard from 6 A.M. to 9 P.M. seven days a week, never made enough money in any one year to pay income tax, but he fed and housed a hungry family of six without complaint. Nor did we feel sorry for ourselves, living by a simple and ancient principle: people were put on this earth for work, horses, each other, and God. In that order.

Save some shoemaker ancestors in the Black Forest of Germany, all of our families had been farmers until our father, Tom, began dealing with work horses, carriage horses, and finally gaited saddle horses. I could put a high-spirited horse through five gaits before I could drive a car. The horse was more difficult to handle, for its soft mouth was more sensitive than a transmission. It was alive.

Father (we always called him "Dad") rented out horses for riding by the hour. In the bad winter days when no one came, we would have a huge basin of popcorn for dinner, surprised that there was butter on it; the butter was a gift from Uncle Charlie, who had a failing dairy farm.

Aunt Louisa, who lived with us, was a spinster, tightly dressed throat to ankle, to protect herself from those beasts, men. She always insisted on saying grace, although Father did not approve (it delayed his eating by ten seconds). She would bow her head with its bit of purple lace pretending to be a cap, bring her skinny hands, which had never known a wedding ring, up to her throat, and pray:

> Mush is rough,
> Mush is tough,
> Thank Thee, Lord,
> We've got enough.

The children — Bob, Alice, Paul (me), and Kathryn, all five years apart — were a scandal to dear Aunt Louisa, for while she said grace each of us would have a hand poised in midair, with a fork if that evening there was solid food, or a bare hand if it was popcorn. Never having had children, she innocently thought they would do what they were told. She said that she would pray for our souls silently.

Work was a magical word in that generation. My first wife, Mary (now dead), and I were married at Oxford and then came home to live with her father, since I had no job. He was a decent, kind man who labored to keep his own family of four kids. After three weeks he asked Mary that bitter question which hundreds of thousands of fathers-in-law have asked: "When is Paul going to work?"

Mary replied, "But he does work. Every morning after breakfast he goes up to our room and writes."

Her father, trying not to despair about his daughter's future, commented, "I know he writes, but when is he going to *work?*"

It is important for you to understand the curious sort of life I — your father or your grandfather — led, because it was unique to this country and it will never come again; you will never see it. But the man of seventy-five whom you see (all too seldom — I despair if you don't come) was made into whatever sort of person he may be by surviving circumstances whose toughness was justified by the smug-sounding remark that they formed character. For years I would get up at 5 A.M. and walk the two miles to my father's barn. There I harnessed two horses to wagons especially built for the telephone company. They had spools of copper wire rotating on rods, pots for heating lead to solder the wires, climbing irons for strapping on the workers' ankles (the men were called "grunts," probably because climbing up an ice-covered pole in winter would make anyone grunt), and the usual pliers, wrenches, hammers, fuses.

Nor have I followed the usual life of the two irreconcilable families from which I come. On one side, the gentle, peaceful Reinheimers who had first been shoemakers and then farmers (in the Black Forest I found their house; over the door, a carved boot and the date 1580), and the Engles, violent, tough horse people who would rather knock you down than finish an argument reasonably. From those two opposites came your father/grandfather, whose compassion fought with his fists. Sometimes the quarrelsome half of his temperament triumphed, and he did foolish things. Usually, the kind aspect won, as in the fact that he has helped, with money and sympathy, more young American and foreign writers than anyone else in this country.

Here I am, coming out of the world of horses, of selling newspapers on the street and delivering them to houses, of clerking in a drugstore with an old-fashioned soda fountain, driving a car for an elderly lady, all jobs done afternoon and evening, seven days a week, after a full day at school or college. The Engles had a gift for working seven days a week and still do—my older brother, when he managed the largest Woolworth's store in the Midwest, did work his seven days, and I still do, at my job and my books, as does my dear wife, Hualing.

In 1932, after graduating from Coe College in Cedar Rapids, I studied and wrote for a year at the University of Iowa for my M.A. degree. In that year I may have been the first person in the United States (or perhaps any country in the world) to receive that degree for an original book of poems, the first "creative writing" degree. Perhaps there were others of whom I do not know.

In 1932 all of my luck—after all of that work—changed. Maybe work makes luck. I won a very large fellowship to Columbia University (which even paid round-trip travel from Cedar Rapids to New York City), the Yale Series of Younger Poets Prize for publication of a first book (I think that since then, if I may be forgiven the remark, more of my students at the Iowa Writers' Workshop have won that prize than have students at Yale), and a Rhodes Scholarship. Never was there such a miraculous year in my life up to then, and never again.

When I arrived at Oxford I had a male "scout" to bring breakfast and lunch to my room, make my bed, clean and shine my shoes. The first time he took away my shoes there was a bit of horse manure on them. When I remembered that, I was embarrassed, but when my scout Bert brought them back, he said, with great pride and respect, "Sir, I see that you have horses." He did not know that I was not a gentleman rider, but the guy who shoveled out the stalls of a poor man's barn and that my father, far from being rich enough to keep horses as a hobby and for pleasure, kept them as a tough way of keeping his family alive.

It was a hard and happy life. We never felt sorry for ourselves, not even our mother, in agony after drinking horse liniment by mistake. But how was such a turbulent and fortunate life possible in the twentieth century? Answer: because I had the luck to be born in the United States. I've lived a long time in Europe and Asia, a valuable and necessary experience. I spent my first honeymoon in the Soviet Union, a tough combination. I lived parts of three years in Nazi Germany, and in all the Communist countries save Albania.

If you do not know another language you do not know your own, said that great manipulator of the German language, the poet Goethe. It is also true that if you do not know at least one other country, you do not know your own. When I comment on the United States, I do so with a certain sense not only of my own country, but also of many countries around the round world, those of the far left, the far right, and the genuine democracies. The latter, alas, are painfully few in the total number.

Why does it matter where you are born as long as you are a healthy child? The difference is absolute: will you have a healthy mind, be allowed to read anything you want, be free to criticize your government, take any job you want if qualified, study whatever you wish, travel anywhere in this country or in the world with a passport which your government must give, be safe from arrest for holding the "wrong" ideas or reading the wrong books, and, with your own dollars, send your kids to schools where they are not required to learn a rigid ideology? All these privileges were given you at birth by this indulgent country. There are few countries of which this is true. We like to think of ourselves as a continent, but in a sense we are really an island in a sea of authoritarian governments, with which you will have to live. Our own system is the oldest surviving in the world. Why? Because of its graceful flexibility. If people are bitter against our government, they have a way of getting rid of it short of violence: at the next election they can simply throw it out on the street (although with fat pensions).

For us the word "free" is natural; it is our right. In much of the world it is seldom mentioned in the press, on the radio, in public speeches, or even in conversations. When socialist countries sign a solemn treaty guaranteeing the rights of free speech and travel, they ignore their written commitment. The same is true of right-wing governments. Hang on to these rights you are lucky enough to have as you will hang on to life itself. Without such rights there is no life. Without them people are only pathetic parodies, creatures wearing trousers, shirts, and a sorrowful face—save when they are ordered to smile.

For many, many years the people of this country could largely ignore other countries, so far away, so little affecting us. Now you will have to worry about what some fool on the other side of the world will do, because today his actions are so close to us and can have so instant a chain reaction. Who knows the fearful world in which your children will live, if they do live? Never before has such a ghastly thought been a part of our thinking. Suddenly mere survival, not so-called progress or pleasure, dominates our future and hangs over our head like a mushroom cloud. We need not only power but imagination, not only to endure but to keep our mortal lives alive.

Hate authoritarian governments, left or right, but not the decent people trapped by them.

When I was a little boy and my father was driving a horse hitched to a wagon, a sleigh, or a surrey, I sat next to him, holding the end of the reins after they had passed through his hard hands. It was exciting because I could feel moving through that long leather length the tug of the horse's mouth and the gentle shudder of the reins as Dad manipulated them. "Drive 'em soft, Paul, or they'll get hard-mouthed and turn into pullers." He also spoke to them in tight situations more softly than I ever heard him talk to my mother.

Kids don't hold the ends of reins any more. Deprived!

Grandpa Jacob Reinheimer had been an Indian fighter in the Civil War, sent west to oppose the Sioux rather than south to fight the Rebs. His favorite remark when we were children and the cousins were pounding each other was, "Now boys, don't fight." He rode endless miles over rough and wild country as a trooper. I have a photograph of him in full uniform, handsome (how the family has deteriorated!), tall, bearded, saber upright at his right shoulder, a horse pistol tucked into his belt. Instead of the standard boots worn by the Fifth Iowa Cavalry, he is wearing beaded moccasins. He looks dangerous, threatening, yet, like most soldiers, he was a peaceful man. He talked about the "Battle of Burnt Beans," when an Indian alert at night caused his commanding officer to order the fires put out, and the kettles of beans were overturned. He once said to me, "Paul, we should have left those Indians alone, instead of destroying their hide wigwams, their little dog sleds, their holy things, and a lot of the people." He collected those wonderful nickels with a buffalo on one side and a noble Indian face on the other. He gave each of us one on our birthday. I could feel the earth tremble as the great herds ran over it. What ape ordered that nickel to be discontinued? It was our history.

I write this out of concern and affection.

This book is dedicated to you and not to my beloved wife, Hualing (is that too old-fashioned an expression?), because I have dedicated to her something more valuable than a book — my life, my life.

Iowa City, 1985

Paul Engle: A Poem

The name Paul Engle trembles on his tongue.
Should it be bellowed, sneered, whined, bleated, sung?
Look at his broken (football) crooked nose,
His shifty way of letting his eyes close
When they look into your own eyes. Too grim.
How could you buy an old used car from him?

Yet as a father what he gave was love.
Yet as a husband what he gave was love.

He likes his liquor, but his hands don't shake.
He talks too much, merely for talking's sake.
He seldom bores you, but he makes you mad.
He is not really evil, only bad.
He likes all animals, dog, cat and woman
(For whom his love is human — all-too-human).
Some think him worse, now, than he really is.
Some think him better than he really is.
His hands still calloused from his working youth,
His brain is calloused bending too much truth.

Eyeball to eyeball, he and his memory stare
As glittering mirrors into mirrors' glare.

Let it be said of Engle in his praise:
He loved his life-crammed, people-crowded days,
The rough of rock, the autumn's hovering haze,
Skin rubbed on skin, the loving, living blaze,
Bird wing far brighter than the air it beats,
Cabbage worm greener than the leaf it eats,
The high hysteria that lies behind
The howling horror of the manic mind.

Let it be stated clearly — he was cruel,
But only to the cruel and to the fool.

He liked to laugh, and yet he laughed too loud.
He loathed the selfish, greedy, and proud
And told them so in language much too flip.
He lost good friends because of too much lip.
Each day his eyes run the fast razor's track,
But see the radiant mirror sneering back.

Still from his father's boyhood barn he knows
The reek of horseshit trotting through his nose.

Engle's sun forgetting to go down,
Burning his body, family, friends, and town.
His mind is loaded like a dirty freighter.
His fighting poles meet at no mild equator.
He can be tricky, he can talk you blind
As you slide across the mean ice of his mind.
He knows that keyhole shame (but will he lie?)
When his brown eye grins back at a blue eye.

A woman's hands were moons that shone like tin.
Stars rose and set in the bright sky of her skin.
With her, the bare boards of the bedroom floor
Melted into the black earth's burning core.

Watch his slick hands whenever he will deal.
Some find him gentle, glad to share a meal,
Others, abrasive as an emery wheel,
Generous with his time, a tender heel.

His nature contradicts his contradictions.
He sinks his teeth in the neck of his convictions
And hangs on while the jealous kick his ass,
Knowing such bitter pettiness will pass.
What he believes, he shouts with too much breath
He'll cry "Imagination" at his death.

Some meeting him think at once, how horrible,
But some (how wise!) think him adorable.

Ask Engle what he thinks of Paul, he'll say:
I'm a real bastard with a beautiful way.
For burning thought, I'll put my hand in the fire
And get down on my knees to blow it higher.
Those who oppose me always hate my guts.
The narrow academics think I'm nuts.
My hand gives you a poem or breaks your jaw.
My head's grown old, but still my style is raw.
I'm a more troubled man than what you saw —
When a cat bites, I stamp on its small paw.
You'll always understand where Engle stands —
I'll knock you down, then hold your hating hand.
I have the slyness of the not too bright.
I can't move mountains, but I can make light.

Quick centuries ago I knew this place,
Lazarus looking with his ghost-gray face.
I envy the skilled sculptor, working alone,
Who puts his passion in the passionless stone.
The past is my bandage wrapped around today.
The bleeding wound of everything I say.

I walk on yesterday's white winter meadow —
Snow casts no shadow falling on my shadow.
I tilt my turning past until it bends.
Broken-down windmills soon become my friends.
Fast at the best, impulsive at the worst,
I drop my second shoe before the first.

Holding a handsome tintype one dead day
I watched grandfather's dark hair turning gray.
Eternity, where Engle memories meet,
Runs raging underneath my running feet.

xxiv Paul Engle: A Poem

Some things I hate and hate them bitterly:
Complaining, whining men of pure self-pity,
Woman who wanders daily not much nearer
To hard reality than her soft mirror,
The hypocrite, without tears, who still cries,
Whose teeth and mean mouth smile, but not his eyes.
Whose arms embrace you in his bold attack
While one hand slips the bright knife in your back.

Some things I love and love them far too much:
The rabbit hopping in its hopeless hutch,
The baby bawling when its pants are wet,
Black cricket chirping till the sun has set,
The man who says — I'm I, but I am yours,
Woman who says — I'm I, but I am yours,
The salt that burns the bitter child's cheek, salt
That stings as child howls, No, it's not my fault.

Although my cunning triumphs by itself,
Sometimes my sneaky way defeats itself.
Although my male physique won't make you blink,
My skinny arms are stronger than you think.
I'll give the time of day, time of my life,
To poets, children, animals, my wife.

I write this poem-frantic, tough, loud, firm,
A cowboy robin wrangling with a worm,
And while I watch the quarreling language squirm,
I drag it up from the resisting ground,
Word against wordy man, without a sound.

At seventy, beat-up, jailed for the crime
Of beating horror, beauty into rime,
I walk the black-out cell block of my brain,
Sure I am mad, but sure that I am sane,
A cornfield kid, crazy for English words,
Old scarecrow lonesome for the screaming birds.

A Lucky American Childhood

F irst memory of Mother: she had taken me to the Linn County Fair at Central City, Iowa, a pleasant place with trees along the Wapsipinicon River. Dad talked with old cronies down at the horse barn and watched the harness races while Mother and I visited the food and sewing exhibitions and talked with Uncle Charlie in the cattle barn where he was competing with his Jersey dairy cows. After a few hours of lemonade and pop (I was only four), nature startled me, and I said, "Momma, I gotta go."

Mother took my hand and led me to the little wooden buildings marked "Men" and "Women." But which? As almost a male, I should have gone to the Men's, but Mother didn't want to turn me loose among the race drivers, farmers, trapeze performers, strange men. She took me into the Women's and led me to a toilet. I stood in front of it, shocked by all the sturdy farm wives lifting their dresses around me, shocked by what I saw, and unable to "go."

"Momma, let's get outta here," I begged, putting my problem back in my skinny shorts. As always, she understood, took my hand, and led me outside. I told her, "Wait," and ran around the corner of the Women's building by a trailer. I was happily making my little water when a tall woman with a tiny pair of shorts and a piece of cloth around her bulging breasts, spangled and glittering in the hot Iowa sun, came out of a tent marked "Arabian Nights Dancers" in wriggling letters. She had red slippers with toes that turned up and back in a circle. "Hey, you little bastard," she yelled, "you can't do that here." Nature fought with fear. I had to go, but I was scared. I went on going. She slapped my face. I continued to go. Then she saw how small I was, leaned over, breasts bursting at the jeweled cloth, patted the top of my head, looked at what I was holding in my right hand, and said softly (I remember it as seductively), "Still, it *is* kinda cute," and went back into her Arabian tent. Recalling her voice now, I suspect she was from south Chicago. In that moment I was introduced to the delicate world of dangerous women. I have had lesser praise since that quick, warm remark at the Linn County Fair on a hot Iowa afternoon by the corner of the Arabian tent. It was the sight of that woman's bare body, not the slap, that stopped me. I pushed my smallness back into my pants. Mother had been standing at the other corner of the tent, too startled to act. She came over, saw that I was properly buttoned up, took my hand, led me to the Methodist Ladies' tent, and bought me a bottle of strawberry pop. I knew that if I drank it, there would be another crisis in an hour, but after an experience like that, a man needs a drink.

I don't remember Mother feeding me, dressing me, bathing me, picking me up, in those first four years, but the simple gesture of making a tiny stream of water on dusty ground with the big voice of a beautiful woman yelling at me was the most dramatic moment of my life until then. The image of that exotic "Arabian" dancer with the midwestern voice still dances in my mind.

My second clear memory of Mother is watching her in a half-size oak rocker combing her long, long hair. From the time she was born to the day she died she never cut her hair, so that in her last years it hung down to her thighs. It was thick, glossy, abundant, shining the more the more she pulled through it her little, black, double-edged comb with its very fine teeth. As she drew it with quick, graceful strokes of her arm, she rocked in rhythm with the comb's motion. I sat in my own tiny rocker and stared at the glory of it, proud of a mother who owned such a marvelous, living decoration. (The lady next door had recently "bobbed" her hair, which had also been long; Dad called her a "bob-haired bandit" because, he said, without her dense hair wrapped around her face, it looked like a revolver.) I had such a miserably small amount of hair that to see so much was to see a miracle. After each day's combing, my mother braided it and then coiled it on top of her head, where it was neat and out of the way, for she had hard, dirty, vigorous work to do.

On the morning after I returned from three years at Oxford, when I came down for breakfast, Mother was rocking and combing, braiding and coiling. I almost wept at seeing again the homely, feminine, beautiful, and, above all, personal act in a private home. I was fresh from hearing Hitler howling at masses of uniformed men in Munich, streets-long columns of Nazi Brownshirts yelling back at him, their right arms raised in that outstretched salute which was not a soldier's recognition of another soldier but a gesture of aggression. I had listened to Mussolini screaming at his Blackshirts in Rome. I had been in the immense line of people in Red Square waiting to enter the tomb of Lenin and look at the short body of that man radiating revolution, the line going up and down the length of the Square many times, shuffling in silence, their eyes fixed on that square block of marble where they begged for comfort and power. Inside the tomb, guards kept everyone moving, fearful that if anyone stopped and stared that person would claim a miracle. I had worshipped with many hundreds under the rose window in Chartres Cathedral, the sun blooming through the many colors of that incredible stained glass and nourishing the crops in the flat farmland around the city. On some of those farms there must have been descendants of the peasants who are pictured in the window. I had watched a motorized German army rushing along a Black Forest road at a speed never before seen in military history, troop carriers with wide benches with soldiers sitting with their arms folded over their chests, their heads up, their eyes lifted, as if they were worshipping the face of their Fuehrer.

Now I was home, in that house where the woman combing the lush strands of her long hair had borne a little boy named Paul. Above us was the bedroom where she had groaned in childbirth and I had drawn my first breath with a human cry.

My third strong memory of Mother is sitting with her in the backyard of our house at 1602 5th Avenue SE, Cedar Rapids, Iowa. We had a cherry tree, which Mother, in a fit of extravagance when she was young, had bought from a traveling salesman who was probably Johnny Cherry Seed. It flourished, gave us a huge crop of cherries each year, which I picked with a short ladder at the risk of my life. (My cousin fell out of the tree when reaching for an especially large cherry and broke his arm, which was set, then had to be broken again and reset because it was crooked; I just assumed that cousins were more awkward than I was.) It was fruit-canning season. I was five. The day before, Mother had cut her thumb deeply when slicing a piece of tough beef. The slash was bleeding again and I was scared, but she took a piece of gauze bandage, wrapped it tightly around her thumb, showed me how to tear the end of the bandage down the middle to make two strips, wrap them around the thumb, and tie them twice. She had a dishpan of cherries on her lap and a big white bowl on the grass by her chair. She would use her thumb to split and "pit" the cherries, then drop them in the bowl. Hour after hour. I helped in my feeble way, sometimes leaving a stem on the cherry, sometimes popping an especially ripe, red one in my mouth.

Perhaps it was the acid in the cherries, or the pressure of pitting, but by the end of the morning her thumb began to hurt. Then Mother noticed that the bandage had turned red. She took it off and found that it had been bleeding badly, dripping blood under the bandage and into the cherries. "Paul, we've got to finish," she said quietly, put the bandage back on, and did not stop until the job was done. We had mother's blood in the cherry pies and jam she made from them. It was a standard morning at the Engle house.

A fourth memory: my brother, ten years my elder, was always called Bob, although his actual names were Charles Glenn Engle (he was named for two uncles, Charles Reinheimer and Glenn Engle, who was of course always called Billie). In the chicken coop in the backyard he had a small flock of bantams, with a fiery, many-colored rooster. It was a special treat for the children when we were given those little eggs for breakfast. One day Bob noticed his rooster moping in a corner, its tail feathers drooping, ignoring for the first time those speckled hens, who must have been so beautiful, so irresistible to him, judging by his rude conduct toward them. His beak was down; his eyes were glazed and sometimes closed;

now and then he would utter not one of the red-sounding crows with which he celebrated the morning sun or his kindness to one of the beauties in his harem but a sad, self-pitying, life-despairing croak. Bob must have been fifteen years old and I five. He came running into the house, crying, "Mama, rooster's sick. We gotta do somethin'. What we gonna do? Hurry. Poor rooster. He's mine. I want 'im."

Mother was cooking, but as always when a child needed care, she turned down the fires and without taking off her apron rushed out to the coop. She looked around with her farm-trained eye, saw that the straw was clean, picked up the rooster's head to examine the usually red comb above his bill and the wrinkled wattles below it, saw that they were pale and that the head dropped down the moment she let it go, and said, "Bob, he needs medicine." She ran back into the house and came out with a bottle of castor oil and an eyedropper. Bob held the rooster so that it could not flap its wings or kick out with the needle-pointed spurs with which he intimidated larger roosters. Small as he was, he would strut around with the hackles on his neck puffed out, lifting his feet like a gaited show horse and swearing at any full-sized feathered creature in his way.

"Now, Paul," Mother told me, "you pinch open his beak." I knew about that, for I had watched Dad pinch the corner of a horse's mouth to make him open up and take the steel bit against which his big teeth had been clenched. Scared, because that rooster had pecked me many times, I pinched. Mother had the eyedropper waiting and quickly emptied it down the bird's throat. Then another and another, the rooster making mutterings of rage, fright, and choking, but we could see him swallow, tilting his head back just the way he drank water. Mother was down on her knees in the filth of the chicken yard, doing what she regarded as the most important thing in life — helping a troubled child whose pet was in trouble.

Early the next day Bob and I ran out to see if the rooster was dead or alive. He was strutting around, clucking what must have been the most shocking erotic comments to his hens, lifting his spurred feet stiff and high, sneering at the full-sized hens and roosters, proud to be a live, feathered male. I don't know how many American roosters have been dosed with castor oil, but our rooster was now a member of the Engle family, enjoying its favorite cure. Brother bantam: I had the same treatment. But I did not strut.

When Bob left home at about sixteen, we stopped keeping chickens, and the coop was torn down. I made a garden each summer where the coop used to be. Its soil was so rich that my flowers and vegetables (half the space went to each) were the best in our part of town, without weeds. I won a hoe for having the best "Victory Garden" in 1918. The judge did not know that it was less my skill than the years of fertilizing by hens, roosters, and Bob's bantams. In honor of Grandfather Rein-heimer and the uniform he wore in his Civil War photo—he was a handsome man with a fine military figure, a black beard, eyes like bullets—Mother had bought me a little child's cavalry uniform. The day the chicken coop was broken up I put on my suit, complete with small sword, and ran around battling the mice that had nested underneath, chasing them with great courage and hacking at them with my dull sword. There is a photograph of me holding my sword the way Grandpa held his and trying to look military and tough.

Eva Reinheimer Engle had been born on the family farm on the northwest edge of Marion, then five miles from Cedar Rapids. The farm was on a hill with oak trees and was called Grand View because from it you could see across the landscape on all four sides. By climbing the windmill, which I did on every visit, including one several weeks long every summer, I could see buildings in Cedar Rapids. Grandpa had received some of that land as bounty for serving in the Civil War. He would sit out in the yard in a chair when he was old and gray and no longer farming, occasionally smoking a cigar.

An old Indian, tribe unknown, showed up at the farm each spring, and Grandpa would give him a room in the barn. He hardly spoke any English, but he could carve anything. One time he took a big cowhorn, pale yellow with a black tip, carved some animal figures on it, and then fitted a little lid so that it looked like a powder horn. Every spring he made me a slingshot out of a tough hickory crotch. I shot acorns in the autumn and stones in summer with it. I can't remember hitting anything but the side of the barn. The Indian helped at odd jobs around the farm and ate with the family in the kitchen every Sunday. When the first frost came, he simply disappeared. One day he was there whittling or shoveling out the cow barn, and the next day he was gone. But in April he would turn up without warning. Once I asked him where he had been. "South."

Eva left the farm when she married Tom at sixteen. I can only guess what happened to that shy and innocent young girl, but I did once overhear Mother whispering to a cousin, "I grew up with beasts on the farm, but I didn't know about men. They're worse."

She was soft-voiced but physically strong. In those days a housewife and mother did not merely spend many hours doing necessary things in the kitchen. The work was hard and often heavy. She did our laundry on scrubbing boards in the basement. Because of their horse smell and often actual manure, she washed Tom's clothes separately from ours, the heavy overalls, the thick riding pants, the sweaty shirts, the wool socks. She carried a huge wicker basket full of wet clothing up the steps and into the backyard where she hung them. That full basket must have weighed as much as a bale of hay, but she lifted it lightly. She could harness a team of horses and drive a wagon. She could climb ladders to pick cherries or to paint the house. She helped spade the garden, hoed it, weeded it. She spent burning summer days in the kitchen canning fruit and vegetables, even when the total savings must have been pennies after she had paid for the Mason jars, the metal tops, the rubber rings. I always hovered around when she was canning to help in little ways, carrying big bowls of skinned and pitted peaches, quartered tomatoes, green beans which had been trimmed and the "string" pulled away, pans of apples which had been chopped and mashed to be made into her apple

butter with its cinnamon tang. All winter I took that apple butter to school between slices of homemade bread for my lunch.
Another reason I always hung around the kitchen on canning
days was that often, when all the jars had been filled, bits of the
fruit would be left and I could eat them.

That kitchen must have been hotter than the hundred-
degree August day outside, but Eva never slowed down. It
must have been a hundred and thirty degrees above those pans
on the stove where she sterilized the jars in boiling water. She
never complained. It was all for the family; what else was life
about? We were devout Protestants who believed that people
were put on this earth to work and to pray. But then, work itself was a high form of prayer, a ceremony of thanking God for
giving us eyes that could see the jobs to be done, and hands
that could do them. Work ordered the world and our lives.
Laziness was a sin like adultery and stealing—it would put you
in hell, a taste of which we had every summer in the heat of
Mother's kitchen.

Whenever she had no urgent work in the house, Mother
sewed. Her medium-sized rocker had a drawer under the seat
which swiveled out from a wooden peg. In it were pin cush-
ions, spools of thread on metal rods, hooks for thimbles, cards
of hooks and eyes, snaps, rows of buttons all in lovely variations of pink, white, gray shell as well as big ones made from
bone or leather (the beauty of buttons has never been celebrated enough in paint or word), binding tape, pinking scissors
with their serrated edges as well as ordinary shears, a cloth tape
measure, a row of heavy needles for sewing buckram linings,
corduroy, denim, all heavy cloth, a beautiful piece of beeswax
which Mother used to harden a loose thread so that it would
go through the eye of a needle. That little drawer was the magical source of the clothes we wore. Mother even made heavy
winter coats. When my older sister Alice graduated from high
school (old Washington High, a huge, dark limestone building
by the railroad tracks, long since torn down), she carried the
first bouquet of roses any member of our family had ever car-

ried and she wore a "Swiss organdy" gown, covered with embroidery and flowers, which Mother had made for her.

Eva also made her own clothes. I shopped with her and learned the names: percale, crepe de chine, cotton suede, tweed, printed cotton challis, muslin, linen. She had an old Singer sewing machine with a foot treadle. I would draw up my little rocker and try to rock to the rhythm of the treadle. Her feet moved very fast, and I would tire long before she did. The needle had to be kept going at a steady and swift pace, hours at a time on some days. I would help her lay the pattern out on the floor with the cloth and hold both tight while she cut out the shapes. A lot of it was hand-sewn: "Paul, sleeves are hardest to fit in. You have to be careful or they will bunch, or get too tight." She once made me a corduroy suit, holding the thick material hard as she fed it under the needle, her feet flashing on the treadle, the bobbin bobbing, the spool of thread unwinding steadily. She knew how to open the head of the machine when thread got stuck inside and to clear it and rethread. Like most housework then, sewing, even with a machine, was physical labor. She had the strong legs of a farm girl, kept firm by miles of walking. When she had to go anywhere, she walked, even downtown to shop and back.

When Mother did not sew, she repaired rips, sewed on buttons. No garment was abandoned until patches began to appear on patches. She once made a "mackinaw" jacket for Bob of wool cloth so thick she had to struggle to get the needle through, as the machine could not handle it. She also sewed horse blankets out of used khaki army issue which could be bought cheaply after World War I. And of course she knit mittens for all of us, usually red with black designs, and sweaters, and things for the feet we could wear around the house in winter because our floors were always cold from our inadequate furnace. She once knit me a green stocking cap with a red tassel. In New York years later I wore it to the Metropolitan Opera House, where a friend had given me a ticket in Mrs. Vincent Astor's box. I was escorted to the box by a uniformed usher who looked in disgust, perhaps fear, at my beat-up stocking cap, maybe the first one ever to enter the "Grand Tier." As the house lights darkened and the orchestra began the life-filled, lyrical overture to the "Magic Flute," I sat in the front of the box, at the gracious invitation of Mrs. Astor, clutching my stocking cap as if it were Mother's hand.

The marvelous voices of the Bird Catcher, Pamino, the Queen of the Night, and the long-sustained melodies of the orchestra flowed through that rough yarn. I was an impoverished graduate student at Columbia University, but in all of that elegance, all those silks and diamonds, I had a greater distinction than anyone else. I had a handmade stocking cap from the needles and fingers of a beautiful lady from Cedar Rapids, Iowa, who did her knitting between moments of washing shirts reeking of horse and cooking cabbages with carrots. It was the only such cap in that glittering "Horseshoe" of famous boxes. I held it proudly, as if it had been a sparkling tiara and (excuse the expression) I had been a beauty.

Mother, you made me a great stocking cap, but you did not make me beautiful.

There was a medicine always in our house, "Sloan's Liniment." Father's constant heavy lifting, throwing bales of hay and straw, and wrestling with the powerful legs of his horses strained his back. I remember him lying on the long wicker sofa, shirt pulled up, while Mother rubbed his back with the liniment, a fiery liquid which must have been mostly alcohol, judging by its smell. I remember him saying, "Ah, right there. Harder." Mother poured another handful from the bottle and rubbed with both of her strong hands.

One winter morning she came down a little after five o'clock and before stirring the batter for buckwheat pancakes she took up a bottle for her tablespoonful of "tonic." It was not tonic but "Sloan's Liniment." We heard her cry and fall. When we ran to the kitchen she was curled up on the floor and writhing as the corrosive burned her stomach. The doctor came and soothed it. Reluctantly, she went back to bed. Her only comment was "I guess I was still sleepy." I still feel the fright, at the age of ten, watching my strong mother twisting in agony on the ugly linoleum floor and Dad bending over her, saying, in the softest voice I ever heard him use, "Eva, you're gonna be all right." Tears were not in his eyes but in his voice. Mother always made the pancake batter the night before so that it was ready. Even while the doctor was looking after Mother, Alice heated the griddle, put on grease, and made Dad his breakfast. We all survived because of what we all did.

One day when I was five Mother decided to make fresh peach ice cream for Father's birthday. We had a wooden keg with a steel tub inside that held two gallons. It had a "dasher" inside connected by a shaft to a crank on the outside. We packed ice mixed with rock salt to make it melt and freeze that rich-smelling mixture with one hundred percent full cream from Uncle Charlie's purebred Jersey cows. Mother poured it in, heaped ice over the lid. The children took turns turning the crank until the mixture became so thick that the paddles on the dasher could not move. When we told Mother that we thought it was done, she said, "Let me try," and knelt down at the crank. As her strong arm and her strong shoulder worked at the crank, she suddenly screamed, fell over, grabbed her stomach and yelled at Alice, "Go get Emma." We knew she was pregnant. The strain of turning the ice cream crank when she wanted it to be just right for Tom's birthday brought on her labor pains. Emma was an old woman living a block up 5th Avenue who "knew about such things." Emma stopped her cooking and ran with Alice to our house—leaving her apron on—and helped get Mother to bed. As she struggled up the stairs, Mother said to Bob, "Try to turn the crank a few more times to make it settle."

We called Father at the horse barn. He was outside teaching a green horse to single-foot, but he rode inside the barn, unsaddled and stalled the chestnut mare, and rode home fast on his bicycle.

We all waited outside the bedroom until we heard a thin cry, which was our sister Kathryn announcing that she was in the world, a member of the Engle family in Cedar Rapids,

Iowa, and that in five years she would be helping us turn the crank on the dasher for peach ice cream on Father's birthday. And joining us in scraping the ice cream, of a richness not known in this adulterated world, from that dasher. From Mother, no complaints, only joy, joy. The blood was nothing. Her only comments after the birth were: "A girl? Good. Did the ice cream for Tom get hard?"

Mother loved flowers. When the chicken coop was destroyed and I made my garden on that enriched dirt, although we badly needed all the vegetables I could raise, Mother helped plant rows of zinnias, marigolds, asters, petunias, salvia, with borders around the whole garden of sweet alyssum and blue ageratum. At ten I had equal excitement from pulling a long carrot out of the ground and from picking a bouquet of flowers for Mother to give a friend. I had a little business supplying flowers for parties around the neighborhood—a quarter for as many flowers as they wanted. Mother liked all colors. I raised wax beans as well as green beans because they had a delicate yellow color, turnips because they were white and purple as well as strong-tasting, red tomatoes but also small yellow tomatoes, golden bantam sweet corn but also "Country Gentleman" because it was white and came late. Looking at the blue, yellow, red, pink, white, orange (nasturtium, with its evil smell), it seemed to me that her eyes became many-colored. Vegetables were like flowers to her.

Those chickens were fun, with their iridescent feathers in all shades of scarlet (we kept Rhode Island Reds), but they were also work. Each morning I went out and gathered the eggs. I had to look carefully in the straw as well as in the nests, because the hens were stupid and often just laid eggs wherever they happened to be. The eggs couldn't be left there because they would go bad. Once or twice a month Mother would come out and pick a hen, or a rooster if we had too many, and say, "Paul, go get that one." I would chase the poor bird around the yard until I had it under an arm so it could not beat its wings, while avoiding the sharp toes. Then I put it in a special little coop with water and feed. When Bob came home he took the chicken by the head, we scattered, and he would "wring its neck," whirling the creature around and around until its head tore away from the neck and the bird fell to the grass. (He always did this brutal act, which seemed to me the height of bravery, on the lawn, so that there would be no dirt in the open neck.) The chicken would flap around in circles, blood running from its neck, still breathing, until it finally lay quiet and unmoving. Then came the nasty part. Mother had put tea kettles on the stove to boil water. She brought out a big dishpan, put the chicken in, and poured the boiling water over it to loosen the feathers, all of which we then had to pick off, even to the tiniest bit of down. The hot water made the feathers stink. When the bird was picked, Mother took a long, slender knife and split its belly, her hard hand tearing out the intestines, but careful to save liver, heart, and gizzard for giblet gravy. That digesting cavity also stank.

Usually in early autumn we bought a turkey and put it in with our chickens to fatten for Thanksgiving. Mother gave it a separate pan of feed. We had a log with two big nails driven in about two inches apart. On the day before Thanksgiving, Bob would catch the swearing bird, tie its legs together, then cramp its neck between the nails, tapping them closer with his hatchet such that the head was an inch or two on one side. Then he asked me, "Ready, Paul?" He nearly always cut off the head with one blow. When he left home to make his own way in a world for which our family did not believe you needed formal education (sister Alice was the first ever to finish high school and I the first to go to college), I took over the job of executing those fowls, not gladly. The first time I made a bad strike with the hatchet and had to hack at the miserable animal's neck several times. "Don't worry, Paul," Mother said, "you'll learn." "Momma, I don't want to learn," I replied, in tears not only at the blood but at the shame of failing. But I learned.

We had a long row of peonies at the edge of our backyard (for reasons I do not understand, Mother called them "pinees"). She went to look at them every day from the middle of May, for each year we had the same question — Will the pinees bloom by Decoration Day? We always waited until the morning of Decoration Day (now called Memorial Day) to cut them, so that, wrapped in wet cloths, they would last longer when put on the graves of the Reinheimer grandparents, Grandma Engle, and little Paul Reinheimer, Eva's brother, for whom I was named. He had died at age eight after pumping ice-cold water over his body at the well after a long hike had made him sweaty. I do not remember any year when we did not have those peonies for our annual trip to the cemeteries in Tom's wagon. We picnicked at the edge of the graves. Grandpa's had a tiny American flag and a star of iron because he was a veteran. We had one clump of single peonies with their circle of huge red petals and a great gold clump of pollen in the center. Each autumn Mother and I took roots from the largest plants and put them in at the ends of the row. They went across the whole backyard and were a decoration to our whole place on Decoration Day, as well as to the graves of ancestors, most of whom I had never seen.

When I was seven years and eleven months old, I began to worry that at eight years there might be some awful power connected to my being named for Paul. I finally told Mother one day that I was scared of my birthday. She said, "Paul, don't worry. You'll be all right." She put an arm around me, and good power flowed through it into my thin shoulders. But when I woke up on October 12, my birthday, I shuddered. Paul was buried by himself away from the rest of the family (I still don't know why) on a hill south of Marion and under great oak trees. I was always the one to put the flowers from our own plants on his grave. All day I was nervous, no good at Johnson elementary school; when I came home, Mother had baked a huge cake, my favorite kind—a layer of chocolate, a layer of green, and a layer of yellow, colored from little bottles she kept on a kitchen shelf and only used for important occasions. It was covered with black walnuts, the richest, sweetest nut in the world, from the grove on the Reinheimer farm. A piece of that cake would kill me today, but at the moment of my eighth birthday it was as comforting as an affectionate hand. Mother had cracked those nuts with their iron-hard shells by putting them on a sadiron and beating them with a hammer, then picking out the meat with a little sharp-pointed pick with elaborate designs; along with other picks and nutcrackers (which were useless on black walnuts), it had been her mother's.

By bedtime I felt that I might really make it. Next morning after I woke up I went down to the kitchen for my buckwheat pancakes and said, "Mama, I'm eight years old and *one* day!" She patted my head and told me what she had not had the courage to say before, "You're just like Paul. He was a good boy, and if he had lived, he would have been a fine uncle to you."

The marriage of Eva and Tom was one of the strangest combinations of a man and woman I have ever seen, and I have been a close and fascinated observer of couples in many places and countries over the brief eternity of my life. Eva was medium height, with a strong and handsome face, that incredible wealth of hair, a warm and hearty voice, and a belief that men and women were put into this world to endure, and to do so without complaint. She was Tom's opposite in every detail. He had a violent temper and would yell at us children for the smallest noise or for the failure to do what he expected of us. Mother, never harsh toward us, had total patience and an absolute devotion to her children, which must have been so intense partly because it was hard to communicate with her husband. Because of the ruthless demands of Father's job—he had to feed and water those great animals twice a day, every Saturday, every Sunday, every holiday—there were ruthless demands on Mother. She envied wives whose husbands only worked five or six days a week when hers worked seven, from six o'clock in the morning to nine at night, and often later in summer.

Mother wanted a quiet life and got instead the neighing of horses and the yelling of horsemen trying to handle those beasts so much stronger than they were. Father asked for the salt at dinner as if he were threatening your life. She had a piano (how did Father afford it?) and played it evenings, singing hymns and old songs I have forgotten, but one about Ireland haunts me still, "By Old Erin's Shore." She wanted all things gentle and got all things violent. She wanted a clean house and got cinders, manure, straw. She wanted quiet and calm language and got instead the obscenities and profanities of the horse barn. She wanted the house to smell good, and she got neat's-foot oil on a harness, the odor of horse urine on Father's boots. She wanted to worship in St. Paul's Methodist Church every Sunday morning but had to stay home and cook Tom's dinner, because Sunday was for him not a day of prayer but the best time for business (many Sunday noons I would take a basket of food from Mother and ride my bicycle to the barn, balancing a dish of gravy and a Thermos of coffee on the handlebars). She wanted to see people but almost no visitors came to our house save relatives. Our neighbors would invite each other for supper or just to drop in for the evening, but ours was a closed house; no one ever came. Mother was outgoing, but her life was ingoing. We were all warned that other kids should not enter our house when Tom was home, because their noise might disturb his energetic reading of the newspaper. Mother wanted people, Father wanted silence. Mother wanted singing, Father wanted silence.

Yet they communicated. They were married for fifty-five years. They accepted hard work, animal violence, rank smells, constant pain, the needs and joys of children, the harsh struggle simply to have enough to eat for six people. Her name was Evelyn, but he always called her Eva. He was completely dependent on her. When she had her first heart attack and was in St. Luke's Hospital, he despaired. Late in the evening of the day she had been taken away, he could not bear going to bed alone. I was writing at the old rolltop desk when he came in. He stood staring at me a while before he begged, "Paul, do something." There was nothing I could do and he knew it, but in his nature he could not speak of feeling, only of action.

In my second year at Oxford, in 1934, I published a book of poems, *American Song*, which was widely reviewed and widely sold. With the royalties I brought Mother to England. Sister Alice left her husband, Vic, a good engineer, to shift for himself and came to Cedar Rapids to cook Tom's early pancakes, to do his horsey laundry, and to listen to his horse talk when he came home. Like Mother, she hated the whole rough world of animals and the tough language that went with it. She told me that the Greyhound bus stopped outside our house to pick up Mother as she left for New York and the ship to Southampton.

I met her at Southampton with Edward O'Brien, the famous anthologist of the annual "Best Short Stories," who had come along for the ride and because we had become close friends. I drove a rented car, for which I was fined by Oxford University because I had not asked permission. In Oxford I had rented a room for her in an ancient, narrow street near Folly Bridge. It was at the back of a house and overlooked Pembroke College. Next morning, Mother said, "Paul, I can't sleep. Look out the window." Below was a Pembroke courtyard paved with old gravestones. They haunted her.

My tutor and rowing coach, Neville Coghill, medieval scholar and former oarsman, a big and handsome man, and a friend of Masefield's (with whom he invited me to lunch), had us for one of those elaborate Oxford lunches, with many fine dishes and several wines, all of them strange to Eva. In her hard Iowa voice, the opposite of those so-English voices around her, Mother talked and laughed and charmed. She did not know about the final "e" in Chaucer, but she did know about the final value of a human being. At the top of a winding, fourteenth-century stone staircase, in a room with leaded windows, a room filled with books whose titles she did not know and in many cases could not even read, surrounded by the cultured intelligence of England, she talked of flowers, children, even horses. When we left, Neville Coghill stopped me and whispered, "Paul, your mother is a great lady." That afternoon he rowed my ass off on the Thames in the Merton College eight. Mother watched from the bank at a place called "The Gut." Afterward she said, "I never saw you work so hard."

When Mother had her first heart attack, she stayed in bed a while and recovered enough to take up her usual life of cooking, cleaning, and walking with our first daughter in her arms, which gave her strength. When she had her second attack, she had to stay in the hospital, unable to speak. Every evening Father and I (Bob, Alice, and Kathryn had married and moved away) went to the hospital; he did his evening chores early, I helping feed, water, and shovel. She lay silent on the bed, her marvelous hair scattered over the pillow. Tom would look at her and ask, his voice quavering in a way I had never heard before, "Eva, can you hear me? It's Tom." Out of her silence Mother would nod her head in a yes. I tried not to think what was going on in the mind of that woman who could understand a voice but had no voice to reply. Such moments are not the tears of things, because they are beyond tears.

We sat in silence until Tom asked, "Eva, are you all right?"

She nodded yes.

He held her hand for the first time in my presence.

She squeezed his hand gently. They were talking.

Each evening he would say, "Eva, I gotta go. Say good night." She nodded her head.

I asked the attending doctor at the hospital to call me in Iowa City if Mother's condition changed. One day Tom called, weeping, stammering, "Eva died. They didn't tell me."

So that strong, brave woman, who loved people, died alone in her lonely bed. She who cherished her children as her life died with no child by her. She who waited each year for the rich and delicate odor of "pinees" died with only the smell of medicine. She who embraced and touched us constantly died with no one there to hold her hand.

I walked home along streets lined with the white wooden houses of people like us, the nonrich, the workers, the baseball fans, the Czech immigrants who loved music and homemade wine, streetcar conductors, the Quaker Oats employees, salesmen, small grocers. In brief, they were the solid people, not really poor but of what used to be called "modest means," among whom our mother lived. She saved a nickel when she could, and so did they. Coming to 5th Avenue and 16th Street SE, I looked at the streetcar tracks leading from downtown up 5th Avenue by our house and ending in Bever Park. One day when I was perhaps ten, Mother went to the dentist. I was mowing the lawn when a streetcar stopped at the corner. Mother stepped out and walked toward the house, holding a cloth to her mouth. When she came close, I saw that the cloth was saturated with blood, and there was blood on her chin, hand, and blouse.

"What happened, Mama?" I yelled as I ran up to her. In a muffled, strangled, almost hissing voice, she said, "I just had all of my teeth pulled." The words dripped blood.

After that draining, painful ordeal she did not take a taxi home, but the streetcar. The taxi cost fifty cents and the streetcar a nickel. Whatever the pain, she was always happy to save forty-five cents for her children. We knew it. Penniless, we gave her the only treasure we had: intense, total, limitless love.

Tom

He was an old horse himself, this handler of horses and any animal: noisy, tough-bodied, no fat, a good feeder, driving himself as hard as he drove his horses and children, twice as strong as his slender body looked, beating his way through the hard world of horses and horsemen, working his fifteen-hour day, seven days a week the year round, selling, buying, trading, always "dickering" for a horse, bridle, saddle, giving riding lessons, renting out horses by the hour to people whose riding skill he despised, shouting at us kids, sometimes beating us, always loving us.

He died in my arms after he fell from the horse he had just been riding.

A tough old bastard who held back his emotions (except for rage if you didn't ride up to his high standard) until they exploded in him, and he wept.

He was born in New York state and brought to a farm near Eagle Grove, Iowa, as a small boy. His father had been an infantry soldier in a New York regiment, captured at Chickamauga and taken to Libby Prison. When someone, usually a naive person who had married into the family, asked the stupid question, "How did he survive Libby?" the answer was quick and clear: "Because he was an Engle. Too mean to die."

Grandfather Engle had married his own cousin. The family belief was that a double mixture of Engle was too much. At least that was the view of the gentle Reinheimer family, from which my mother came. They were a turbulent outfit, those Engles. Grandpa, after the Civil War, after Libby Prison ("Those Rebs were sorry they captured him," an uncle said), stayed a while on that Eagle Grove farm. Tom's toughest memory of the place was a great windstorm which drove a straw through the wall of the barn. It was a typical Engle act: if there are two ways of doing something, do it the violent way. Then Grandpa went west and ran a store for miners in Leadville, Colorado, in that beautiful valley where the hills glowed inside with silver. The Oklahoma land rush came, and

Grandpa galloped across the line into that empty, rocky, hopeful landscape, and into emptiness, into oblivion, for his family. He never wrote again. They did not know if he was dead, remarried and with a new family, arguing in the stubborn Engle manner over a piece of stubborn ground, killed in a fight when some stranger yelled back at him, "Say that again, you bastard, and I'll beat the shit out of you," and he said it again, no hesitation. He was an Engle.

One day Tom got a letter from the War Department asking if he was the son of a certain veteran of the Union Army who had just died at an "Old Soldiers' Home" in West Virginia. Father's name, it said, had been found among the "effects" of the old soldier. It was the family way. You didn't ask for help, in a tight spot you shot your way out, you took no crap from anybody, and you would rather die alone facing the empty air of eternity than ask for help, sympathy, a crust, or a dollar from anyone, and, above all, not from a relative. A pathetically few scraps, including a piece of paper with Tom's name and address, were sent to us. Grandpa had been a part of three of the great American experiences: the Civil War, the farming of the Midwest, and the last opening of a western frontier. He died alone, among strangers, too proud perhaps (it is an Engle trait) to write to his own son. I never met him.

By the time he was sixteen — he never finished any school — Tom had a job in Oxley's livery stable at Marion, Iowa, on the edge of Cedar Rapids, grooming, harnessing, feeding, watering horses, cleaning equipment, washing buggies which salesmen, just off the Milwaukee trains a short distance away, could rent for their calls. He drove trotters and pacers at county fair racetracks, but when he married Eva from the old family farm on a hill outside Marion, he moved to Cedar Rapids and opened his own barn. He bought, trained, and sold carriage horses, then work horses, then saddle horses. He also drove fancy horses in the show ring, "high-steppers" he called them, in classes called "roadsters." We had a stack of blue, red, and white ribbons that he won. He had an absolute skill with horses. Riding young and not-well-broken horses, he controlled them not with blows, although he carried a riding crop, but with mutterings in the throat, wordless appeals, threats, approving grunts. Horses would lay their ears back not in anger but to listen. They understood. Within a week of arriving, a new horse would learn his secret language. I have seen him simply go up to a horse which was rearing and kicking, stand in front, say nothing, catch those great eyes with his own gray eyes, and wait in silence while the animal settled down. Then the sugar lump, and the horse would nod its head up and down in thanks.

Tom was the only person I ever knew who could train a cat. Any animal which hung around our barn got trained—stray dogs, a raccoon, a pigeon he taught to eat from his hand. Our cat was mixed, white paws, white tip on its tail, black rings around its eyes. Nothing, not even rope, is as flexible and as hard to make stiff as the backbone of a cat, but Tom taught that animal to sit up straight, front paws out, and beg like a dog for food. We had buckwheat pancakes for breakfast in winter, wheat in summer, every day forever. Mother would always bake two extra ones called the "cat pancakes." Tom took them to the barn. The instant the cat heard the car door slam she ran out, purring, rubbing against his leg, looking up to see what was in his hand. In the barn, he would tear off a piece of pancake, hold it out at arm's length, and wave it back and forth. The cat would watch it with cunning eyes, walk back and forth a few times, then suddenly jump into the air, snatch it with the needle-pointed claws of one paw, squat down on the floor, and nibble at it like a dog with a bone. If I went near her pretending to take away the scrap of pancake, she would growl at me deep in her throat. Then another piece, and another, until the two pancakes were inside her swollen gut. She washed them down with a pan of milk and went to sleep it off on a bale of straw. Sometimes Tom would tease her by not showing the pancakes. Then she would sit up straight, tail out behind as a balance, and sound the equivalent of a dog "speaking." Dogs are impetuous fools compared to cats. Once she was on a bale of straw when a mouse ran by on the floor. She waited until it was exactly the right distance away for a silent leap, claws on all four paws cutting the quiet air.

One winter day I helped Father harness a team to the bobsled. He went off to a farm a few miles away to look at some baled straw and hay. Not just look, but smell. The nose tests hay and straw. Tom could sniff a bale, predict what it was like on the inside, take a hatchet and cut the twine binding it; when it fell open, there were the texture and quality he had prophesied. I have seen a farmer praise his baled hay, its color and freshness, but Father would take one quick smell and say, "Yeah, looks good, but it's moldy inside." The farmer would protest, but when the bale was split, there was a center of smelly mold.

I went off to my paper route, and when I came back all hell was breaking loose in the house, doctors arriving, my brother and sisters huddled close to each other in the living room, and in the bedroom Tom was lying on the bed groaning, his whole body battered, blood over his face, his chest, and the bed. His left arm was twisted. He wavered between awareness and unconsciousness. When he drifted back into seeing us terrified at the door of his room, he cried out the old Engle shout that came without thought from the marrow of our bones, "Get the horses, damn it, get the horses." The effort would throw him back into silence and closed eyes.

Slowly we learned what had happened. He had been driving along the country road on his way to look at, and smell, the hay and straw in a farmer's barn before buying it. He was driving the team at a smart trot (he always had better, racier, jumpier horses than he could afford) when the bobsled hit a hump of ice and bounced up. The horses reared, throwing Tom from the seat out under the rear hooves of the horses, who bolted down the road. Both the front and back runners, thick, heavy, steel-hard, juggernauted over his thin, light, steel-hard body. He lay in the snow, knocked out, bleeding.

A farmer coming down the road saw the runaway team, stopped it, drove them back until he found Father, loaded him in the straw covering the floor of the bobsled, then drove him back to his own house, helped his wife hitch up horses to his own bobsled. Together they had driven into Cedar Rapids to our house. Today, bodies are taken directly to hospitals, but in the teens of this century you brought your injured home.

If he had to be broken and in agony, Tom wanted to be home. He always said that hospitals made people sick. He was never a patient in any hospital. He only spent one afternoon at St. Luke's Hospital, when I carried him in my arms through the emergency entrance after his first heart attack at the barn. If he had been conscious, he would have kicked and cursed me for not taking him home. After his second heart attack, he would have hated those hours in a hospital room before he was declared legally dead. I wanted him to swear at me in his old horse language and order me to take him home. I wanted him home, his clothes stinking from that great odor of horse-urine-manure-hay-straw, his suffering mouth speaking my name in horse.

My nose remembers the complicated smells of our house on that day when a stranger and his wife brought our beaten father home: drugs, Father's barn-smelling clothes, Mother's stew of cabbage, carrot, cheap beef in the kitchen (life had to go on, kids had to be fed), the smell of neat's-foot oil rising through the hot-air ducts. How boring the clean smell of a modern house.

He recovered from the accident, but only after some weeks in bed, which he hated and took as a personal insult. He wrestled that bed as he would a horse, twisting, turning, swearing, beating it with his fist. We children stood outside looking through the door, afraid to get too close. Father had a leathery voice and an instant temper; when he lost it, he yelled at us with a sound like the crack of a buggy whip. Even injured, an invalid in bed, he was violent. He dealt with us as he did with horses. If we did something wrong, it could be corrected by howling cuss words and giving us a smack (sometimes many) on the bottom, so that we howled back. It took a harsh voice and a hard hand to control an unruly horse, and Tom did not change his habits from barn to house. The most casual remark about food or weather or a small household incident or a disliked relative was not spoken, it was shouted. Our house not only reeked with strong odors, it also rang with strong sounds. Some of that noise was the howling of us children when we were punished for committing an Engle crime: being loud when Tom was reading the newspaper or taking a nap, not shoveling snow from the sidewalk at once after a storm, not cutting grass on the lawn in time (when it was higher than the heavy toe of his shoe), not arriving at the barn after school to throw down bales of hay for feed and straw for bedding as fast as he thought we should. The horses kicked him, he kicked us.

One day my sister Kathryn, five years younger than me, pulled open the kitchen drawer too far while Tom was taking a nap, and it fell to the floor with a terrible clatter of silverware, startling him awake. She ran and hid under a table while Tom charged into the kitchen with his right hand raised. Kathryn was shaking while he looked around, muttering, "Damn thing couldn't come out by itself." When he found the criminal, a spanking ensued, with more howling.

We not only feared that man, we loved him. No father ever worked harder for his family. He was up at 5 A.M. every day of the year and off to the barn by 6 A.M., full of pancakes, syrup, sausages, oatmeal. Since the horses had to be fed and watered twice a day, he always went back to the barn in the evening, seldom coming home before 9 P.M. In the summer he rode a bicycle the two miles each way; in winter he walked in the snow. Our noon meal was called dinner, not lunch, for it was the biggest table of food. A man who had been working six hours tossing bales of hay and straw, shoveling out wheelbarrow loads of heavy manure, training horses, riding miles with people to whom he was giving lessons, often having walked four miles, needed meat-potatoes-vegetables-bread-butter-pie, and lots of them. The evening meal was supper, less than the noon food but still heavy, still a lot. Because of his sloppy eating habits, Mother always put newspapers under Father's plate to protect the tablecloth and catch his drippings. This often resulted in a dramatic performance as he read items in the paper that delighted or infuriated him, on which he commented wildly. One day he said, "Hell, I've read this one," got up from the table, furious, stretched out on the wicker couch in the living room and read the *American Horseman* with snorts of agreement and indignation.

His newspaper reading each late afternoon was also a vivid performance. Home from hard work, shoes off, in his shirt sleeves, he heightened every news story with excited remarks. About a politician who had been caught with both feet in the public trough: "Serves the bastard right. Throw him out." Of a teenager accused of petty theft, and glaring at us: "Kids ain't what they used to be. No respect. Oughta take a rawhide to their ass." Of a long excerpt from a flamboyant preacher's sermon: "Betcha God gets as tired of hearing that crap as I do." When an item made him really mad he would shake the paper as if it were to blame for the world's errors and sins that it was reporting, stamp his feet on the floor as if those humble boards bore the guilt for the follies of men, women, and governments, look up at the ceiling as if it were a heavenly cloud with singing angels, and yell at the world as if it were a rearing horse: "God damn it, I can't take any more of that. The world's going to hell in a handbasket." He read all the comics with explosions of laughter, slapping his thigh and reading them a second time for the second fun. His response to a crime story was enthusiastic and plain: "They oughta hang the bastard." The pages about "society" and fashion he read with snorts of contempt and cries of "Thinks she's so fancy! There's things she does just like the rest of us." Sometimes he would get so angry he would throw the paper down on the floor, get up and stamp around the room shaking his fists and beating up the air because the politician or crook who had enraged him was not there. It was exhausting for all of us when he read the evening *Gazette*, but he made me a newspaperholic.

Our house had been built by a carpenter who was a friend of Father's. He designed it as he went along, so that it had odd little closets where he had not planned well. There were two in the kitchen, one in which Tom kept his outdoor coats and his shaving satchel with straight razor, leather strap, mug of soap, and a brush of bristles. It smelled of horse and enriched the cooking odors. There was an entryway from the back door where Tom had to take off his dirty boots before coming into the house. There was another little closet with a door where Mother kept her sewing things and Father a brown metal box with mysterious papers that we were forbidden to touch. Years later, after his death, I opened it and found a mortgage on the house and bills for loads of hay, oats, corn, straw, saddles. There was a little spiral notebook in which he had entered the names of the horses he had rented out and the amount received for each day:

Ginger	$1.00
Dorothy	$1.00
Joyce	$2.00
Prince	$1.15

There was a deed for two lots in Cedar Memorial Cemetery. He had buried Mother in one, and a year later we buried him next to her. There was a bank statement with a pitifully low balance. The box was always locked, but the key was on a string tied to the handle.

The stairway to the second floor was protected by a solid wooden railing; we used to slide down it whenever Father wasn't around. He didn't worry about our falling, only about the wear and tear on the wood.

Money was the great mystery in our lives. We never knew how Father survived. Some days his income would be two dollars, and six months of the year he could not rent out horses, for only he and I ever rode in the intense cold and snow. He was so frugal that even Mother had to beg him for enough money for groceries so that he himself could eat. It was humiliating to see her ask, and to see how reluctantly he gave her a dollar. When she was brave, she would say, "That won't be enough, Tom. I want to buy some meat today." Then a half dollar would appear. And yet he would do strange, unexpected, generous things. One day he came home with a phonograph, with a little crank. Winding it was my job. There was only one record at first, "The Dance of the Sugar Plum Fairies," and we played it over and over until next month he bought another, "Poet and Peasant Overture." I never did learn what brought the poet and peasant together or what they talked about, but if it was animals or crops, our family could have given the peasant some lively talk. Through a miracle, we took a vacation each summer, sometimes renting a cottage at the "Upper Palisades," high limestone cliffs along the Cedar River some miles below Cedar Rapids. We would drive there in an auto filled with sacks, bags, groceries, bedding, pans, kitchen things, my books, sewing materials, usually a cat or dog, and the kids under all of that. We never knew how Tom paid for it, but it was a daring adventure for the children. We would walk along the edge of the cliff as close as possible to see who got dizzy first. There were snakes in the woods and even swimming in the river, fossils in the limestone, cornfields close by where I would go in the evening and borrow a dozen green roasting ears. One time the big white farm dog was in the field and chased me home, he barking, I yelling for Dad to come out of the cottage and save me from those slavering and furious jaws.

Some summers we would camp out in a tent by the banks of Indian Creek east of Cedar Rapids, driving there in a big wagon with a foot of straw on the floor, pots and pans, knives and forks, a bread box, rubber sheet for the ground inside the tent, tough clothing, an axe (for the wood we had to chop to make the fire for cooking), towels, everything needed for survival in a grove of hickory, oak, and elm trees by a clear stream with a sandy bottom and a deep hole where I learned to swim. It must have been hell on Mother, who had to leave a comfortable enough house to sleep on the ground and cook on a sheet of iron. On the way to the camp we would watch for metal signs advertising tobacco and other household items. When the kids saw one on a tree or telephone pole we would yell out, Tom would stop the team, and we would run over and tear it off. Our favorites were advertisements for "Clabber Girl Baking Powder" (imagine being Miss Clabber Girl of 1917) and

"Horseshoe Plug." That was our cooking surface, after we had burned off the paint. The kids caught crawdaddies under logs in the creek, walked miles on sandy roads gathering wild daisies, always barefoot, squishing the warm sand between our toes. One year we took a two-seated buggy—a "surrey"— piled high with all our camping things, my sister Alice (five years older than me, so that would have made her about four- teen) sitting on top of everything. The horse reared up when a dog came out of a farmyard barking. Alice fell off and the rear wheel passed over her. She was an Engle: she got up, beat the dust out of her dress, and climbed back on top of everything. We grew up knowing that life was tough and getting run over was a natural part of it.

One night it rained hard, and Tom got everyone out with the axe, knives, and pans to dig a trough around the tent so we would not be flooded. The kids loved it; Father cussed and shouted orders. Mother endured, as always. When the job was done, Tom surprised us by laughing as he said, "Never figured this family would turn out to be ditch diggers." Then all of us crawled back into the tent on the wet pads to spend the rest of the night, while thunder cracked in the trees overhead and lightning flashed through the tent to show our sleepy faces full of the joy of camping.

The next night a cow got into our food box and ate every- thing in it that appealed to cows.

One day, swimming in the deep hole of Indian Creek, I was bitten on the cheek by a small snake. My face puffed up, and I could barely speak; Mother put me on the pad in the tent and applied hot-water compresses to my face. They worked, and I have been talking without interruption ever since.

In winter there was less to do at the barn, although the horses had to be fed and watered twice a day, and blanketed, and the manure had to be shaken out of the bedding straw and new straw put down to replace the dirty. On Saturday after- noons Tom would announce, after dinner, that we were going to the Majestic Theatre or Greene's Opera House, where we saw vaudeville (Chinese performers sliding down a wire from the top row of the balcony to the stage by hanging from their queues; we called them Chinese pigtails). Were not "The Desert Song" and "Alice Blue Gown" played there, while my ears were ravished by what seemed the most glorious music in the world and cruder parts of me had shameful thoughts of ravishing those actresses in their sparkling gowns? Comedians later to be famous played there. Father loved the confrontations, the songs, the color, the lights, and when the villain was punished in the end he would beat his big hands and cry, "Let 'im have it! Let 'im have it!" How did he get the money for that indulgence in the winter of no income?

When he was courting our mother, Tom worked for a judge in Cedar Rapids, caring for his horse and buggy and being of general use. He had long curly hair which Mother admired; it was one of the reasons she was attracted to him. A few weeks after their marriage his hair gradually straightened out, and she discovered that this tough horse guy had been curling it nights for so long that it looked natural. Watching him expertly shake out the horse turds from the unsoiled straw and pitch it with a long graceful swing into the wheelbarrow, I tried to imagine him after a hard day's work in the barn looking in the mirror and putting curlers in his hair.

Fourth of July in those days was a violent event, which seemed just right for the Engle family in the violence of our lives. Tom always found a little money to help out the nickels, pennies, dimes we had saved from selling newspapers and doing odd jobs. He worked tough hours for the cost of the firecrackers, tiny ones called "ladyfingers"; in a burst of extravagance we would light the end fuse and watch the whole string writhe on the sidewalk as one after another burst open and shook the others. There were nightworks, which were our favorites, because Father would be home from the barn and could help shoot them into the black sky where they made a child-delighting (and apparently Tom-delighting) flare of flame. One time Father took a Roman candle, held it up over his head, lit the fuse, and it backfired along his arm, burning a path from hand to shoulder. We waited for his rage. Silence. Then he looked at the children and shouted, "Anybody does a dumb thing like that, he's a God-damn fool." He stalked into the house. But he had spent his little money on that show, for us kids.

Tom was short, wiry, loud-mouthed, profane, terrible-tempered, uneducated but clever, keeping every emotion under control save anger. He was wonderfully shrewd about animals. Let a horse be led by him, at a walk and a trot, let him run his hands over the body and legs, open the mouth and look at those great teeth, stare into the large, liquid eyes, watch the movement of the ears, the nervousness of the hooves, the switch and carriage of the tail, the snap of the hocks in the show ring, the instant response to a horse trader examining the soul of the creature as well as its bones, and Tom Engle could tell you exactly the strength and character of the beast.

There were people who found Tom a shrewd listener to their problems, a sympathetic ear in a horse barn when they could not get so compassionate an ear in their own, less earthy homes. He could express his own feelings to outsiders more easily than to us inside the family. Yet his devotion to the family was total. His response to news that what I was doing late at night on my old rolltop desk (which I had bought from a neighbor for ten dollars) was writing poetry, astonished and excited me: "I had an uncle who lived with the Indians in Michigan, wrote poetry. He published some books. Later he lived in Dowagiac. He was a friend of the official Indian at the World's Fair in 1893." At Oxford University in 1933 I was in the Bodleian Library, that ornate, handcrafted, dark yet colorful, ancient but used-every-day place where books are like warm bodies in its Thames-valley-cool air. They speak back to you; they like to be touched. Going through the catalog, huge volumes of handwritten entries, I found the name Engle and the titles of the legends in verse that Great-Uncle Engle had written. They were Tom Engle's pride. How did they get from the Ojibway country of Michigan, the great woods with deer running and wolverines trotting and ducks flying from lake to lake, to this city where the medieval and Renaissance mind of England was massively, beautifully carved in stone?

Tom was an intelligent man who happened to handle leather saddles and steel manure forks instead of books or machines. He had total skill with animals and little with his family. I have seen him pat our mother gently on coming home at night and two minutes later yell at her, "God damn it, woman, I told you what I wanted." He handled horses better than he handled his children. We all lived in fear of him and his burning temper, at the end of which was his hard hand. He was kind in his own harsh way. Do what I say or suffer. He could make animals respond as he wished; why shouldn't his own children do the same? Or his own wife? Especially was his relationship with Mother complicated. He admired her, he cherished her, and he hurt her deeply. He would come home full of the day's story, the slick trade, the sale of a horse he wanted to get rid of, the improvement at cantering of Ginger (our favorite, a big-boned gelding who had a rough canter), the price of oats, the purchase of a western saddle with fancy stitching to use for "greenhorns" (he despised anything but a flat "English" saddle of polished pigskin), the house shaking with the loudness of his voice. Then he would find a small thing not the way he had expected, the food not cooked just the way he wanted, or his favorite cushion missing from the sofa, and that dreaded roar would hit Mother: "Why can't a man have things the way he wants them? I work my ass off all day, and what do I get when I come home? I'm out there slaving for this family, and all I ask is to have things done the right way."

Mother would sit at the dining-room table, not eating the food for whose preparation she had sweated in our hot, tiny kitchen, tears falling down her cheeks and into her empty plate, watching Tom stuffing himself while dripping onto the newspapers under his full plate.

She mended his ripped pants, sewed buttons on his shirts,

stitched up tears in his coats. There was a lot of that repairing, for Father's life was rough not only on his skin, muscles, and bones, but on everything he wore. His way of life dragged her into crudities she loathed, but she never wavered in supporting him.

When Mother died, my sister Alice came to live with Tom, get up in the predawn blackness to cook pancakes for him and his cats, and sort the accumulation of objects from fifty-five years of marriage. One evening she got out the box of Christmas decorations to see what should be thrown away. There were delicate globes from the Black Forest and "cornucopias," little horns made by the kids with Mother's help from scraps of wallpaper. They were hung empty on the tree on Christmas Eve, and by morning they were mysteriously filled with candy. Father was sitting on the floor with Alice. When he saw those simple ornaments he and Eva had shared for fifty years, he put his hands over his eyes and cried, cried into the night.

Tom had a heart attack when he was seventy. It came at the end of a day when he had thrown a hundred bales of hay, eighty to ninety pounds each, up over his head from a wagon into the hay mow. After Mother's death he did everything with wilder energy. He was so lonesome for her, he filled his days with such a turbulence of action that he could not think: riding horses for hours on the excuse he was "getting them on their gaits," painting the barn, repairing stalls, breaking a green horse, shoveling out a ten-foot-deep manure pit and selling the well-rotted stuff to ladies for their flower beds, pitching the powerful stuff over his head into a wagon, standing at the bottom of the pit raging for the death of that woman. I saw him put tears instead of spit onto the handle of the pitchfork to get a firm grip.

He was ill in bed for a few weeks, once again beating the covers, howling at God and the doctor; his idea of taking things easy was to pound the ribs over his painful heart. Gradually he strengthened, and the doctor said he could do light work. "Hell," Tom told him, "I've got chores to do at the barn.

There ain't no light work. There's people who work and there's bums." So he went back to the barn that was his life, lifting the bales, the ears of corn, the pans of oats, the saddles, the heavy pails of water. One day I came from Iowa City, where I was writing poetry and trying to teach it, because I wanted to take a long ride. Books build a wall against life; I wanted to sit on top of the great, round rib cage of a horse, put it through its gaits, feel those legs slashing out in a sharp trot. Tom was already riding King in the cinder ring when I arrived. He pulled and yelled to me, "I'm still workin' on his trot. I'm gonna take him down and bring him back at a good clip. You get down and watch whether he goes square."

Father clucked to King and went, as he would call it, "sailing" down the cinders. As he turned at the end and headed back toward the barn, I saw him touch King lightly with his braided leather crop. I crouched down and watched the lovely horse legs coming at me. I could not hear Tom's voice, but I could see his mouth moving as he coaxed and soothed and gentled with sounds more comforting than he ever used to his children. King was going great, his legs true and straight. Four feet from me Father pulled up, stretched King out, and asked, "How did he—?"

Tom took a sudden, shattering breath, looked at me with amazement and love, and fell from the saddle. I caught him in my arms. King was a good horse. He never moved. He was a Tom Engle horse.

My first reaction was an ashamed feeling—how light my father was. That right arm had burned my bottom so hard, I had always believed there must be a big man behind it. He was small, he was helpless, he was dead. I did what I knew he would want. Before putting him in the car for the drive to St. Luke's Hospital, I took King into the barn, took off saddle and bridle, led him into his stall, haltered him. He had said to me while in bed after his first heart attack, "Paul, if I can't ride a horse I want to die." He committed suicide twice, once by overworking after Mother's death and again by violent riding when his heart was frail. As he turned away from me on that last ride with King he shouted, "I'm gonna make this the greatest horse we ever had, God damn it."

He died like an Engle: swearing, in violence, in love for my mother, in whose death he died.

The Drug Scene

Although many people have regarded me as a jerk, one of the titles I remember most warmly is "soda jerk."

The change from the rank and (I believed) blood-enriching odor of horse manure at Father's barn to the delicate fragrances of perfumes, at the drugstore where I worked many years late afternoons and evenings, was natural. They both delighted the human nose. I spent seven hours a day, seven days a week, for seven dollars a week, in that little place crammed with drugs, lotions, tonics, tobacco, candy, ice cream, ointments, soft drinks, writing papers, newspapers, magazines, and the row of pumps with their many flavors called a soda fountain. That is the precise word, "fountain," for a push on the knob marked sarsaparilla, strawberry, or chocolate brought a lively squirt of concentrated taste. Then a push on "soda," and the effervescence foamed up around the scoop of ice cream in a tall glass, and some lucky kid had a "soda." Now, of course, the drugstore culture has deteriorated—real drugs instead of a soda fountain!

The counter was marble, with a pattern of little fossils circling around others. I played those flavor pumps with their rich syrups as if they were the console of a spacecraft. To prove that I was a professional, I wore a long white apron and a white shirt with the sleeves rolled up, like a doctor who had just scrubbed for an operation. The boys in my class at old Washington High School would bring in their girls, and I would serve them sodas, or "sundaes," big globs of ice cream with chocolate or fruit syrup, or "banana splits" with even more ice cream, syrup, and nuts. They sat in a corner at little tables with those wonderful chairs made of twisted heavy wire. Earning my buck a day, I had shameful envy of the fact that they had allowances every week and all that free time between school and supper. Even today, fifty-five years later, I cannot meet them, now gray, paunchy, comfortably middle-class, on the streets of Cedar Rapids without that old sense of jealousy. We smile at each other, we talk warmly, and deep in my evil heart I think, "Okay, you bastard, I served your girl friend, whom you brought there grandly in your old man's car."

An old-fashioned neighborhood drugstore was a window into the whole area. I knew who was sick because of the prescriptions my boss, a registered pharmacist, filled for me to deliver, whose baby had a fever and needed a thermometer and orange-flavored little aspirin, what bearded old man drank female tonic for its alcohol (it was Prohibition), what husband bought prophylactic "rubbers" by the gross and had me charge them as toothpaste. I knew the gray-haired grandmother who drank "Elixir of wine, iron, and quinine" on a prescription that never ended. I used to take the cork out of the gallon jug in which it came and smell the rich odor, from which I received as strong a charge as she did from drinking it. There was the big Swedish streetcar conductor who stopped on his way to work every day and bought a nickel cigar; he broke it in half and put one piece in his mouth to chew and the other in his pocket. When I rode the streetcar I always sat as close to him as I could in order to watch his dramatic performance. If you chew tobacco, you have to spit. In the floor next to him was a hole covered with an iron plate flanged so that he could step on it to open it. Then he would take an iron rod and put it between two rails to change the direction of the car. But often while still handling the moving car he would step on the cover to open it and spit an amber stream with the precision of a pitcher throwing a baseball. He never missed. We all have our heroes.

There was also the minister of a Protestant congregation which believed that tobacco, like alcohol, was an instrument of the devil. He would come in, buy a ten-cent cigar—a Harvester, named for a famous racehorse—and go into the back room (where I had a chair and a tiny table), light up the weed, inhale, and sit back in the chair, holding it out in front as if it were a sacred chalice from which he had just been blessed. His face, round, red, had the beatific expression of a believer who has just had a vision of choiring angels. "Paul," he would say, his words sounding smoke-colored, "never tell a lie. Just don't let anybody know about my seegar. It's my only sin." He preached at the funeral of a friend. I wondered if his prayer to the Almighty had less effect because it smelled like a ten-cent cigar.

There was a middle-aged bachelor around the corner. One day he brought in a prescription, leaving the bottle every week for a refill. "Paul," the boss said, "every time you touch that bottle go wash your hands." And that was how I learned about venereal disease.

There was the stooped old lady whom I called Aunt Tillie, although she was no relation. She came the first day of each month to buy a copy of *True Story* (regarded as too daring; my mother wouldn't let it in the house) and a bottle of one hundred aspirin. Her hands trembled so badly that I had to write her check, which she would then sign in a shaky and hardly readable script. Tired from her walk of several blocks, she would always sit and rest at a table. I brought her a glass of ice water. She sipped as if it were a rare imported brandy. Then, if no one else was in the store, she confessed. "Paul, my father was a smoker. Do you know something?" She leaned closer, as if what she was about to say would mean a fall from grace, as if it were too wicked for the ears of a young kid. "Mama hated that pipe. Sometimes she hid it, but I knew where and I'd sneak it to him under a newspaper, because I loved that smell. He used a tobacco that smelled sweet and so did the smoke. Now wasn't that awful of me?" Sometimes she talked about her children, who all lived far away. "Had a letter from Mary today. She thinks Ed, that's her husband, he's a traveling salesman, is carrying on with another woman. I wrote, maybe so, but Mary, you're a complainer. Men hate 'em. Spruce up, treat Ed real friendly when he comes home. Pat him. Men are just like young dogs, they like to be petted." I looked at her quivering hands and thought of them, smooth, warm, patting a returned husband. Her eyes watered. "Paul, get me some more water. I need an aspirin." Then she took two.

When she got up to go she passed the cigar counter for our

shared ritual. I slid back the glass door, she leaned over, sniffed the strong, brown odor of cigars and blocks of chewing tobacco, sighed for the pleasure she would never have, and said, "Paul, isn't it awful of me?" Then she tottered back to her solitary little apartment, her stomach full of aspirin, her nose of tobacco smell, and her mind of the "true" stories she would read that evening. She always patted me as I held open the door.

Then I went back and soaked with water from the soda fountain the two big sponges we hung in the cigar case to keep the cigars moist, taking a good long drag of that forbidden air.

I worked long hours and I worked every day, but I loved that store, where I sometimes felt more at home than at home, knowing where every tiny item was kept, all of the strange tonics whose labels listed strange chemicals, exotic barks, odd flavorings; the shaving creams, soaps, and brushes (men used a bar of soap in a mug stirred with a bristle brush in those days and a leather strap to hone the razor, a glittering piece of dangerous steel); the beauty aids, which were mostly bought by women whom no artificial help could make beautiful; the briar pipes polished until they were as smooth to the touch as a woman's skin. I was a universal boy in a universal store.

There was the large-bellied, large-voiced, large-shouldered construction worker who came in every Sunday morning for Bromo Seltzer to cure his indigestion and hangover after his regular Saturday-night binge. He would walk in gently, as if the floor hurt his feet and the pain went all the way up to his head (looking back, I suspect that it did), bellying up to the soda fountain as if it were a bar in the wild west, and say, "Paul, the usual." I would serve him that bubbling, effervescent, hissing glass. He would toss it down to his bubbling, effervescent, hissing gut. A moment of respectful silence, then a belch like an organ tone shaking the glasses on their glass shelves. He would look at me and say in confidence, as if we were equals and I also had belted too many slugs of bad whiskey the night before, "We had a real barn burner." Then he would hitch up his pants, which were slipping down over his swollen stomach, bang his glass on the marble counter until I thought it would shatter, and shout at me as if I were a hundred yards away instead of only a hundred inches, "Hit me again, Paul." He dug foundations, he put up buildings, he poured cement, he carried heavy planks, shaped forms, sweated in summer and froze in winter, never complained, told his male jokes ("Paul, you're too young. You wouldn't understand. But there was this woman . . ."). I used to see him plodding home from work, his shirt filthy, his shoes covered with mud or cement, his weary chin on his tired chest (it shocked me to see that he had definite and not small breasts), working and walking his solid way toward the Saturday-night bash. He, and millions like him, built this country. It was an honor to serve him a bubbling Bromo.

The drugstore was one half of a square wooden building at the northeast corner of 4th Avenue and 16th Street SE. One half was butcher shop–grocery store with an apartment on the second floor where the family who owned the building lived. Some days when I went to work Mother would give me a shopping list for Jack, the butcher. Like the owners of the building, he was Czech, but he had picked up an English nickname. To be Czech was to be one of so many storekeepers in Cedar Rapids in the early part of the century, and that meant to be honest, hardworking, friendly to kids. Some of the new arrivals chopped the English language as if it were a side of beef on a butcher block, but we communicated. My note usually had a note at the end, "Jack, please throw in a chunk of liver for the cat." The Czechs were great sausage makers, and Jack had a smokehouse behind the building, with a pile of hickory wood alongside. Days when I would be pumping a small bottle of castor oil out of a gallon can, the smell of wood smoke enriched with fat would drift through the back door, and I knew Jack was smoking sausage. He would also make what we called Bohemee bolognee in rings, the first time I ever tasted garlic, which we never used in our Iowa-farmer kitchen. I used to sneak out and get a slice of garlic bologna like a drunk sneaking a snort of booze.

There was a small barn behind our building, where Jack

kept a tough horse named Jack for deliveries of groceries and meat around the neighborhood. No matter how busy I was in the drugstore, when I heard Jack the butcher going out to harness Jack the horse, I had to run out the back door and watch, because it was a battle of champions. When Jack the horse heard the barn door open, he went wild, rearing up, kicking the plank walls, baring his terrible teeth, his huge lips curling back, his whinny a savage threat yelling, "I'll break every bone in your body. Get outa my way."

Jack the butcher never yelled back. He would pick up the harness from its peg and walk slowly up to Jack the horse, calling to him in that soothing tone my father used for his own hard horses, muttering Czech words I did not understand mixed in with "Come-on-a-Jack. You-me friends." Then he would open the door into Jack's stall and stand there a moment, his small round eyes staring into Jack's huge oval eyes and chanting, "Come-on-a-Jack. You-me friends." The horse would lunge around his stall, lashing out with his legs, snapping those great teeth, rumbling in his throat deep tones that sounded to me like Czech words. Then he would pass too close to the butcher, who threw the bridle over his head, slipped the bit between his teeth, put an arm over his neck, and growled, "Attaboy, Jack. Take it easy. Attaboy, Jack." His arms tough as leather, he would slip the leather reins over Jack's back. Suddenly he had control, the animal settled down, walked out to the wagon, backed into the shafts, let Jack hook up the heavy leather tugs, twitched his skin, snorted enough to prove his self-respect, and accepted the plain fact that he had a job to do. When the wagon was loaded with groceries and meat, Jack the horse became another personality. He knew all the stops, he knew where he would be given a lump of sugar, where he would be called by name: "How-are-you, Jack?" He was a great conversationalist. When someone called out to him, he would whinny his savage cry out of his yard-long throat, stomp the street with his steel-shod hooves, showing what a good boy he was to bring them their supper. As Jack the butcher drove out of the barn with Jack the horse, I went back

into the drugstore, out of the animal life to the perfume
counter. That was my toughest and most voluptuous job.

The drugstore had a row of heavy flasks with various perfumes. The stoppers were "frosted" so that they needed twisting to remove. If a lady (females were "ladies" in those days,
and fifteen-year-old boys were taught to call them that)
wanted to know what a certain fragrance was like, I would pick
up the bottle, shake it gently, then slowly take out the stopper,
and, with what seemed to me a romantic gesture, wave it back
and forth under her nose. Some of them leaned forward to get
a closer sniff, and as I poured the fragrance over their nose
their breasts would pour their pear-shaped elegance over my
eyes. I didn't get that sort of marvel at the tobacco counter.

My problem with perfumes was to get them out of the big
flasks and into tiny quarter-ounce and half-ounce vials without
spilling any. Even a few drops on the floor meant no profit for
that sale. I developed a very firm hand and a cautious eye.
Sometimes the boss would call me over to do the pouring for
him. Professional pride! It was with those perfumes that I
learned my first French words: Essence de la Nuit (I never
knew that night had its own smell, but perhaps it referred to
the lady and not the dark), Odeur Fatale, Parfum d'Amour. It
was all exotic and erotic.

One lady came every week. When she smelled a perfume
that attracted her, she would take the stopper from my hand
and rub it on her dress, "Just to see if it clings, Paul." Each
time she wore a different outfit, so that over the months I must
have kept her whole wardrobe delicately scented. And let the
shocking truth be told—there was a girl from my class at
Washington High School with long black hair and deep brown
eyes who used to visit the drugstore often, pretending to buy a
magazine or a soda, but always lingering to talk to me. When
the store was empty, I would get a perfume flask, shake it, take
out the stopper and rub it behind each curved ear. It was a
more exciting experience than certain more complicated adventures with ladies I have had since. I stole perfume in that
way from my boss.

But I do not think he would have cared, for he was a kind and generous man. "Quite a looker you had there, Paul," he would say after I had sold one of the graceful round vials of an especially expensive perfume. "I saw how she smiled at you. I think you just made a killing." Then he would wink at me, man to man. I was not merely shy around the ladies, I was downright scared, but the boss always pretended I was an adult male and dangerous to all females. Alas, even when I became an adult, that was, sadly, not true. But my ego grew like corn in August, fast and green.

The boss made some things himself. In the basement there was a small gas stove where he would melt down bars of chocolate, stirring in white cocoa butter, which cut the strength of the dark brown chocolate but saved money. He would also blend together glycerin, rose water, and his secret ingredient, gum tragacanth (my Latin studies told me that it means "goat thorn," with the same root as tragedy; I still can't imagine why). The gum thickened the lotion and bound the other elements more tightly. He bottled it under his own label, and once again my job was to pour it from the kettle into small bottles without spilling any. He also made ointments with heavy vaseline, camphor, phenol, rose geranium oil, a dash of cheap perfume, and another secret ingredient, beeswax. This I would stir on a little marble slab with a spatula until it was smooth and buttery. I would carefully fill round metal boxes with the ointments and put on his label. He sold them for less than the commercial lotions and ointments. People would come in during the winter and say, "Skin's gettin' dry. I want some of Jim's hand lotion." Nothing delighted the boss as much as hearing a demand for his own handiwork. But then, he was a happy man, taking life easy, making a little money, playing golf in the summer, puttering around the basement of the drugstore creating his products in the winter. At six o'clock every afternoon he would call to me, "Paul, you better go eat now."

Every morning on my way to Washington High School, about a mile away, I would stop at the store, and the boss would give me a large leather envelope with the previous day's cash and checks in it. Because the school was only three blocks from his bank, I would carry the envelope with tender care (and with a lot of pride, for was I not being trusted?) to my first classes, then during my free hour I would go to the bank for the deposit, feeling like a real businessman as I waited in line with people who ran shoe stores, furniture stores, groceries, garages. A lot of that money I had handled myself at the cash register the day before. Now and then the evening *Gazette* would carry a story about a drugstore being held up late at night. The boss always told me, "Paul, some son of a bitch comes in here with a gun, don't argue. Open the cash register. Let 'im take everything. Then call me after he goes. No talk. Those guys don't like conversation."

After the perfume and tobacco counters, my favorite place was the magazine rack. By the time I began to work at the drugstore I was writing poetry and reading everything. The boss (I learned from a friend) was proud of this. He ordered magazines knowing they would never sell but that I would read every page. There was *Transition* from Paris, where I first read James Joyce and the poet Éluard and others who later became famous. There was *Poetry: A Magazine of Verse* from Chicago. Not one copy was ever sold, but in it I read T. S. Eliot, Carl Sandburg, Edgar Lee Masters, Ezra Pound. Once in a while the boss would pick up one of these strange magazines, read a little, put it back on its shelf and comment, "Well, Paul, I don't know about that stuff, but I guess it won't break any of your bones."

I usually had free time between customers, especially on cold winter nights. The boss gave me a little table in the back room and an ancient wire chair, saying, "Paul, work yourself when you have to. Nobody around, go on back and write yourself." Like Dr. William Carlos Williams, I wrote on the backs of prescription blanks. (One reason why so many of Williams's poems are quick jottings: he wrote them between a patient's birth pains, on the handiest piece of paper.) Much of my first book of poems was written there between the safe and the shelves with their gallon jugs of tonics, the bottles of pills available only on prescription, the poisons and narcotics like opium, whose sale had to be entered in a register, the big metal cans of glycerin and castor oil with a pump on top for filling small bottles. Once I mixed them up and gave glycerin to a man desperate for castor oil. When he found out the next day, he came in and purged himself of a coarse and obscene vocabulary I had never suspected so mild a person knew. My ancestry was questioned, barnyard substances were shoveled into my tender ears (but I recognized them from Father's barn), my future as a criminal was prophesied, the glycerin was dumped in the soda-fountain sink, and my burning customer drank four ounces of castor oil from a tumbler that I had flavored with peppermint. Happily, he left the store and headed home before those interesting chemical reactions took place in his troubled gut.

The steady customers were my favorites, for I came to know them closely, year after year, their health problems, their taste in candy, ice cream, tobacco, magazines, tonics, lotions, shampoos, their operations and hospital sufferings, marriage troubles, their anxieties about children. There was one wife who came every week. We had an understanding. I knew her husband as a tightwad who even hated to give her enough money for groceries so that he could eat. He insisted on charge accounts because then he could see exactly how she spent every penny. She was a handsome woman with glittering red hair, a full bosom, a small waist, and a graceful walk. (Long dresses hid a lady's legs in those days, but I had a hyperactive imagination and could define on the blank wall of my mind just how beautifully tapered her "limbs"—as my modest maiden aunt would have called them—really were, under her skirt.) I would give her one dollar from the cash register and then write in the charge book a phony purchase, magazine, hand lotion, whatever, always without speaking to her about money. Her eyes were ashamed when she took that dollar bill, stuffing it furtively into her purse as if the engraved figure on it were an obscene photo and not the solemn face of an American president.

There was the stocky, ruddy-faced man with shoulders (as Father used to say) built like an outhouse. He seemed to me the greatest spender of them all, for each evening he came and bought a fifty-cent cigar, in those days an amount of money as powerful as his thick wrists. (Do I remember correctly that the cigar was called a Ben Bey and that the box had on the inside of the lid a many-colored illustration of a fierce Arab sheikh on a handsome horse rearing up on its hind legs? I could hear its whinny in the desert air of the tobacco case.) He had the presence of quiet wealth, for he always paid with a silver half dollar. He reached for the fat cigar like a ruler reaching for his scepter, holding it to his nose for a long sniff, rolling it around, admiring its solid shape, the rolled leaves, and then he reached into his vest (flowered, a sure sign of elegance in those simple days) and from one of several small pockets drew the half dollar and quickly snapped it through the air toward me with a cry of "Catch, Paul." I was ready. I never missed. He never asked for his cigar. I knew what he wanted, and the moment he entered the drugstore I pulled the box out of the cigar case. It was a perfect understanding. Years later I discovered that he was not rich; he had an unhappy life at home, and his buying that noble cigar was his way of proving that an ordinary man could have an extraordinary pleasure.

There was an eternal flame at the drugstore. Near the tobacco counter a thin pipe came through the floor to a height of five feet. It had a polished metal cap on the top with two slots. Inside was a pilot light that never went out. By pushing a little knob, more gas was fed up the pipe, and the fire doubled in size. There was a machine where you could clip the end of the cigar at the end where the leaves tapered and were twisted over each other so that no air could come through. But my customer would take from his vest pocket his own pearl-handled clipper, fastened on a shining chain to a buttonhole, and cut off a tiny bit of the cigar. He put the clipped end in his mouth as if he were taking a holy wafer in church. Then he leaned toward the pipe, held the blunt end of the cigar in the slot, and inhaled deeply, pushing the knob so that the doubled fire lit the rich leaves until they glowed. Holding the first smoke in his mouth, he lifted the cigar close to his eyes, admiring the vein in the leaves, the lovely light brown color.

Carrying it gently as if it were crystal and might break, he would go to one of the little tables where I served sodas to the lucky kids who didn't work after school, sit down on a wire chair, unbutton his vest, close his eyes now and then (whenever he inhaled), and puff slowly, making one cigar last almost an hour, seeming to regret each inhaling as much as he enjoyed it, because every puff brought that beautiful stogie closer to that final disaster when it became too short for even one final drag. He not only watched the blue smoke curling up, he leaned forward, because he could not bear to let it go, and caressed it with his nose, inhaling it a second time, so that each cigar became two. We never spoke to him unless he spoke to us. A person celebrating a religious rite deserves respect.

When at last he could not puff one more time without burning his lips, he got up slowly and walked across the store, carrying that slimy cigar butt like a chalice whose use in the ceremony was now over. Then he dropped it tenderly into the spittoon, with an apology, no doubt, for crowding it in with stupid cigarettes, worn-out quids of chewing tobacco, matches, and the spit from ordinary cigars. Buttoning his vest, putting on his fur hat (I always remember him as being there in winter, which made the warmth of a burning cigar seem more important), he would walk out into the night, toward his unhappy home, toward those twenty-three hours of sleep and boring work before he came back to smoke again a ritual cigar. At the door, he would say, "See you, Paul. Don't take any wooden nickels."

Horseshoe Plug chewing tobacco came in solid bars wrapped in lead foil. One of the privileges of my job was that I could keep the lead foil. When each bar was cut up and sold (there was a special slicing machine for cutting it), I would wrap the lead foil in a ball until, over several months, it weighed several pounds. Then I could sell it and keep the little money. For someone who didn't use tobacco, I lived a full life with that weed.

There was the fiercely religious old lady, tall, built like a football tackle, her hair massively swept up into a coil with a tortoiseshell comb on top, who came in every week, with a handshake that should have crushed the bones in my pathetically smaller hand, and gave me her newest anti-nicotine pamphlet, "Tobacco, the Beginning of the Descent to Hell." I tried to explain to this primitive force that I neither smoked nor chewed but only sold what the customers wanted. Her reply was simple: "But if you sell, you are an instrument of the devil." She was the first fanatic of my life, and I was delighted with our relationship. She was hooked on candy. After lecturing me (the effort obviously made her hungry), she would buy a miniature box of miniature chocolates and sit at one of the soda tables, the wire chair disappearing under her missionary zeal. With a stack of pamphlets on her left and the candy on her right, she reached out with her long, fat fingers and popped a tiny chocolate into her large mouth, her bitter sentences sweetened by candy.

Aside from a delicate nose wounded by smoke, why did she fight this one-woman campaign in all the drugstores of Cedar Rapids? Well, the candy counter was never far from the tobacco counter . . .

Crisis was a part of the drugstore's life. Some nights a doctor tending a patient in a neighborhood house would call in an emergency for an urgently needed drug. I called Jim, who rushed over to the store and stayed there while I ran to the house, picked up the prescription, waited while Jim filled it, then rushed back to the house, often in deep snow. (Streets weren't plowed much in those days—horses could go through anything save the deepest drifts.) Then Jim would ask me about the disease or the accident. At all times I knew the disasters of the neighborhood, who had pneumonia (a much commoner illness then) and was in grave danger, who had pneumonia and was improving, what child had diphtheria (so many did back then) and was on the edge, what child was coughing its lungs out, what woman was in labor (so many babies were born in the home then, as my sisters, my brother, and I were) and had been for two hideous days, who had been kicked by a horse or had broken an arm falling from a ladder or broken a leg when run over by a heavy wagon, what house had smallpox and a yellow sign on the front forbidding me to enter (I put the medicine by the door and fled), who was back from the hospital after an operation but, as we said, "was doin' poorly." I knew where there had been a death before the black crepe was hung on the front door. Now my neighborhood looks so clean and healthy because I simply don't know all the menaces, injuries, and illnesses surely present in those quiet houses.

There was the recurring crisis of the intense and anxious man striding in hurriedly and then waiting until the other customers had gone. I knew by the strained and eager look on his face just what he wanted before he took me into a corner and whispered, "Paul, I need a box of rubbers in a hurry."

The first time that happened I replied, "I'm underage, not allowed to sell them."

My customer was destroyed. It was ten blocks to the next drugstore, and with ten blocks back, that meant a heartbreaking delay (two broken hearts, counting the lady who was certainly restless in her room). He began to jiggle up and down on his toes, drumming the glass top of the cigar counter with his fingers.

"Come on, kid," he urged. "I got somebody waitin'."

"Sorry," I said, "the boss wouldn't like it." That was a lie. The boss and I had never talked about those mysterious items high on a shelf in back. I was ashamed at using this tiny scrap of power over an adult with a fever, but I still enjoyed that adolescent malice. A kid of fifteen doesn't often have a grown-up man begging.

"Look," he shouted, "quick, before anybody comes. I'll give you an extra buck. No time."

"I'm not supposed to touch them," I replied, with what must have seemed a smugness certain to arouse the urge to kill.

I have seen desperate men all my life, but this customer was one of the greatest. He was tenor in the church choir, and I had heard his fine voice rolling over the aisles in the old Methodist hymns whose melodies are still bouncing around in my head. No song now. When he opened his mouth, his words were hard as tooth enamel.

"I'll make a deal. Just show me where they are. I'll pick 'em up myself."

That was a fast-thinking hymn singer. I had made the mistake of telling him I could not touch them, not that I could not sell them. Anyway, the boss enjoyed the hymns played on the cash register. My little sense of smug power turned into sweat and ran down my legs into my shoes. On that cold evening, in the presence of an erotic man with a beautiful singing voice, I learned one of the lessons of surviving this life: know when you're beaten.

"Okay," I muttered, and led him into the back room and pointed at the sacred boxes. He took his dozen and after he paid me he put a half dollar on the counter, saying in a lyrical voice, "There, you little bastard, you just gypped yourself out of half a dollar."

He fled into the darkness, jostling an elderly lady at the door. She was a faithful member of his church. If she had known what he held in his tense hand, she would have screamed at the touch as if hellfire had burned her skin.

The ice-cream cans were surrounded with cracked ice on which rock salt was poured to melt the ice and make a colder container. The man who brought them every day was another of my heroes. He had been in World War I and had picked up scraps of French along with some lurid stories about leave in Paris. Once he told me about a French girl whom he called "Sinkunt Franks." I thought it a beautiful name until I began to study French and found out that "cinquante francs" was not her name but her price. He was burly, with arms tough enough to carry one of the heavy ice-cream cans in each hand. I could hardly lift one with both hands. He would tamp down the chipped ice and the salt with a wooden rod, talking all the time to me as an equal. "You know, Paul, some of these gals like to pretend they don't love it. Just hang in there, buddy, and in about five minutes they're going to shake your bones, they're going to be howling. Of course, you gotta work that five minutes and don't get so damn sudden you explode. If you do that, they'll slap you because they're mad." This was a rhythmical speech to the steady drumbeat of the tamper on the ice. While he talked about the risks and pleasures of sexual heat, his hands were in the ice.

I didn't understand all of that wisdom, but I did have a special interest in his Saturday-night visits. He would park his beat-up Chevy outside, come in, belly up to the soda fountain he had been servicing all week, and order two chocolate malted milks. I put in extra syrup and extra ice cream in honor of his connection with our drugstore. Then, not needing to be told, I would take one malted out to the girl I knew was waiting in his car. Not always the same girl, which startled me. I thought that "going with" a woman was like marriage, you had just one. Leaning through the car window farther than was necessary to transfer a cold glass from my hand to hers, I looked quickly at her figure (Engle, you voyeur) and then hard at her face. Did she pretend not to like "it"? Did she howl after five minutes? Did they use a watch to know when it was the right time to do whatever they did and to make whatever noise they made? I was shaken with the idea that those quiet, smiling young women, their bodies bent so gracefully on the car seat, who spoke to me in soft voices, might have a moment in their life so intense that I could not recognize them. In ten minutes I went back for the empty glass that I had carried out full as if I were bringing champagne to a French courtesan. There were even bubbles from the blades of the shaker on which I had made the malted.

One evening I lingered too long with my head and shoulders through the car window staring at a voluptuous creature.

She had eyes darker than the night, but warmer, as she asked, "Did you want something, Paul?"

You're damn right I did, but I didn't know what to call it, and even with the right name I wouldn't have had the courage to suggest it. I ran back into the store where the ice-cream man was bouncing his silver quarter on the marble counter. "Paul," he said softly, because there were other customers, "I been around. Makin' love is like fightin' in the trenches. Take time. Hold your fire. Then let 'em have it. The big gun goes BOOM."

He walked out with squared shoulders, at an infantryman's measured pace, ready to do battle in that most glorious and complicated and eternal conflict, a man with a woman.

The life of my southeast Cedar Rapids neighborhood poured over me, in that small drugstore, like spring rain, warm, close, rich in its abundance of a small-income people. It was a lucky job, doing simple things to comfort the complexity of life. People came in with sprains, bruises, colds, diarrhea, constipation, belly ache, itching skin, headache, dandruff, no energy (they usually called it "no pep"), female problems. They described their symptoms to the boss, because in those days of the early twenties people only went to doctors for the worst ailments. He would listen with a professional nodding of the head, "Yeah, yeah, I know," and prescribe one of the endless cures made from herbs, bark, flowers, seeds, chemicals. He never lost a patient.

I liked going to work, putting on a long starched apron as proudly as a marine sergeant his dress uniform. At the end of the evening, having sold tonics, balms, plasters, cigars, sodas, and magazines, and written poetry on a prescription pad at my tiny table in the back room, I was never eager to go. The boss trusted me. I took the bills, coins, and checks from the cash-register drawer to the safe, stowed them in a compartment, twirled the knob to lock it, hung up my apron, turned out the lights (usually someone ran up at the last minute for some desperate need and I turned them back on), and locked the door. The boss told me always to leave a few dollars and some coins in the cash register, and leave the drawer open, so that if a burglar came in at night he would find a token amount of money, which might keep him from wrecking the place. He was a great boss, and he deserved a better end than death. But don't we all? The memory of that drugstore is a drug against the evening news.

News and the Boy

Why was the bloodiest, most horrible day in English history a joy to an eight-year-old boy on the streets of Cedar Rapids, Iowa, in the summer of 1916? July 1 that year was the first day of the Battle of the Somme in northeastern France. Between sunrise and sunset the armies of England suffered a shocking, unbelievable sixty thousand casualties. In slow and vulnerable lines, under heavy packs, the bravest and brightest youths ever assembled in that green island walked into barbed wire and massed machine guns, under full observation even before they left their own trenches. Every man was a volunteer. They walked straight. They lay dead in straight rows.

That summer I was selling the noon edition of the *Cedar Rapids Gazette* on 3rd Avenue, downtown. In those days the paper would publish an "Extra" if there was some great event, bringing it out between regular editions. I bought them for one penny and sold them for two, a fine capitalist rate of profit. Extra papers meant extra pennies. I would howl out the headlines, "Biggest Battle in France, English and Germans! Thousands Dead! Read All about It!" My voice must have been quavering, uncertain, shrill, but I sold those Extras. My pocket became heavy with little copper pieces because the blasted fields of French farms became heavy with the bodies of England's most loyal, most courageous young men. Every one a volunteer, including the Newfoundlanders, so far from their own loved island.

Seventeen years later, a lucky American Rhodes Scholar, I walked up a circular staircase in Merton College, Oxford University, to meet my tutor for the first time, the poet Edmund Blunden. I had asked for that college and that tutor because I too, in the opinion of hideously prejudiced friends, was a poet. It was rare for an American to know in advance of arriving the names of any tutors, but I knew Blunden's poetry, much of it about World War I.

Wearing my short, black commoner's robe, I knocked on his door. A firm, soft voice said, "Come." In the gray light of the room, darker than the gray morning outside, I saw, in a chair much too large for him, a small, slight figure. Apart from being in the presence of a far better poet, I was doubly humbled, for here was a survivor of the Battle of the Somme, from which I had earned my extra thirty cents on a hot Iowa sidewalk. What I was yelling to the peaceful people of Cedar Rapids to make them buy the *Gazette*s under my arm had been the resolution in the face of terror of that man, a young officer on the Somme. I was ashamed. His pain had been my profit.

His poetry was full of the birds, streams, landscapes of rural England; coming from that gentle air, he could write with gentleness, "Among its broken spades and empty tins I found a pair of boots, still containing someone's feet."

There were no vast battles that winter of 1916, and no Extras. I waited restlessly for summer, when once again the horror of massacred Englishmen would make headlines, and I would bank another thirty cents in the tiny account which would ultimately get me to college and finally to Oxford, although I could neither think nor dream of that at the age of nine, as I was in 1917. I had not long to wait, for "Third Ypres" came, and Blunden was there in the mud under a cataract of German shells, not complaining when he was spattered with other men's blood. I was on the streets again, shrieking. Blunden did his duty, and I made my money. In my hard Iowa voice, I said, "Sir, I have read *Undertones of War*. I liked especially the poems."

In that cold gloom, in the dark Thames valley under its usual clouds, his eyes burned like star shells. Softly, warmly, he replied, "Bless you."

No one had ever before spoken like that to this newsboy. I could feel the *Gazette*'s headlines about Ypres like raised letters in my hands.

My corner was a good one. I caught the workers from the Quaker Oats plant coming off work at eleven in the morning and the new shift on its way in, many of them from the large

Czech community in Cedar Rapids. Some were recent immigrants, with small English. Every morning I sold a paper to a round-chested, thick-armed man who always wore an undershirt for a shirt. He would hold out a handful of change to me and say, "Take," then slap me on the back with a Czech-accented laugh. One day he looked at the coins in his palm and asked, "One of those is a nickel, don't it?" He always opened the paper and read the comics before going on to work.

I was lucky to have so many good smells in my life: horse manure at Father's barn, oiled leather harnesses, Mother's fresh-baked bread, starch on the shirts she ironed herself, the roses she raised in the backyard, the scent of horse that never left my father's clothes, the musty-rich odor of the old leather-bound Bible in German, brought from "the old country" with names, dates, births of ancestors we never knew written in a mysterious script.

If some almighty power were to say to me, "Pick any smell you want and I will send you a bottle," I would ask for the fragrance of a newspaper ten seconds from the press. It has body and liveliness, and there is nothing like it. A hundred perfumes have only subtle differences, but fresh newsprint bulls its way through all of them, putting black ink on the fingers and a quick woodsmell in the nose. But there was one perfume I will not forget; it was rank, warm, sensual.

Several of my regular customers lived in a hotel on the bank of the Cedar River, across the street from my corner. Every morning at ten-thirty I would take a paper to their rooms and hand-deliver it to the women who lived there. Often they would still be in bed, which to my innocent mind meant that they must be filthy rich, royalty, or privileged because of their beauty. We had an understanding: "Don't knock, dearie, the door's never locked."

Entering those rooms was going into a magical cave. There were garments strewn on chairs at which I was afraid to look, but I did sneak a glance out of the corner of my eye. Lacy underwear is not my bag, but at the age of eight or nine I had never seen such elegance put on the human body. The woman in bed would hold out her arm for the *Gazette*, and I would thrust it toward her as if we were transferring a sacred object. (Even today I would argue that the news of the world in an honest Iowa newspaper is a sacred object in comparison to most of the news people read in this desolate and prejudiced world.) Sometimes our hands would touch, and then I would recognize that most intense odor of my childhood: woman, bed, sleep, others who had been in that bed, fresh newsprint, and too much dime-store perfume.

They were open, free, generous, kind, indulgent people. Often they would pay me more than the two cents for the paper. Three cents! I was in business. One day I was given a nickel, unheard of, revolutionary, a wild profit. As she gave it to me, the woman said, in a voice which implied that friendship might mean more than sharing a sled in winter or shooting marbles in summer, "Paul, come back when you're older."

I ran out of that room because it was too exciting. I had just earned more money on one newspaper than ever before: bought at one cent, sold at five. But I also had in my hand a buffalo nickel that seemed alive, roaring, kicking, and likely to horn me in the guts. And it reeked of that powerful perfume. I held it to my nose. In spite of having a shaggy buffalo on one side and an Indian who had lived on that animal's meat and hide on the other, it seemed to me like a woman's skin, seemed to smell like it. That was the largest payment I had ever received, but it burned my hand. I ran across 1st Street and out on the 3rd Avenue bridge. Below was the black water of the Cedar River. I threw the nickel hard, with a snap of the wrist (I was baseball catcher at old Johnson School). It sailed up and then slowly down in a beautiful arc like a woman's arm. Did it really smoke a little as it hit the water, or was that just the tiny foam of its splash? I knew what it was. I looked at the palm of my hand to see if there was a blister. To tell the shameful truth, I have experienced that shrill and moving odor many times since, but never has it overwhelmed me as in that sleep-sensuous room. Maybe because on all the later times I did not have a bundle of fresh newspapers under my arm. To those who need help in those circumstances, I urge a bunch of news-papers with their own seductive smell. Preferably the *Cedar Rapids Gazette*, although after all these years it may have lost its sexual magic.

The newspaper building was on the Cedar River next to the 1st Avenue bridge on its southwest corner. The presses were below ground. Off the press room was a dark area used for storing rolls of paper. It was usually half empty, but for us newsboys it was full of risk and danger and torment and pride, for it was there that Alex Fidler (his real name) held his boxing school. That was where we hung out while waiting for the pa-per to appear. Alex was in charge of all the newsboys. He had an average man's height but twice the speed. Every movement was quick. He sparred with the air. He refereed matches, often running around the ring faster than the boxers. But it was his tongue that had what sports writers call "blinding" speed. He controlled as tough and disorderly and control-hating an outfit of teenage boys as a so-called civilized country held. In the hours before we got our *Gazette*, Alex took our natural vio-lence and gave it order and meaning with boxing gloves. I was probably the worst. By the time I had the gloves tied on and lifted them, I was too weak to hit anyone. Once a Czech kid knocked me across the room and into the wall so hard that I couldn't get up for the funny lights in my head. Alex treated me like a pro, pretending that the leather of the gloves wasn't really tougher than I was.

"Now Paul, hook an' jab, hook an' jab. That roundhouse is for railroads. Keep movin', keep your gloves movin', watch his hands. Soon as you can see, you'll be okay."

Alex kept in shape by keeping us in shape. He cared about us, especially the kids from broken, unhappy, poverty-line homes. If a kid got in trouble, Alex headed for the police sta-tion, where he hooked and jabbed and feinted with his tongue until the boy was free. In that dingy room he was an average man handling smaller kids; in the ring he was a little guy telling fighters who could have broken his jaw what they could and could not do. He taught me two lifelong lessons: when you're knocked down, get up, and whether you are dealing with professors, publishers, in-laws, poets, used-car salesmen, or teenagers, watch their hands—and their eyes. All this I learned, sometimes beaten to tears, in the basement of a newspaper building.

Selling papers on a street corner was great, in the midst of men, women, kids, dogs, cats, horses, and cars going by on the street and on the sidewalk, the whole shuffle and prance of life, the handling of small coins, the sense of holding the events of the whole world in my hands.

Yet I really preferred being a carrier boy in the late afternoon, because it was a family matter. On my route I knew every house. Over the years I delivered the *Gazette* on 4th Avenue SE from 15th Street to 26th Street, the end of the city; I watched the kids grow, the new flower beds blossom, the changes in dogs (always a special concern of the carrier boys), the houses staying the same but families moving in and out, the women who saved a slice of cake for me, the man who gave me an old baseball glove, the houses where, on Christmas Eve, I always knocked on the door and handed in the paper instead of throwing it on the porch as usual, for these places had a small gift, a dollar in an envelope, a necktie, a bag of candy. Delivering a newspaper is different from delivering an order of groceries or a prescription drug, it is more personal, it brings in the events of the world, local happenings, births, deaths, divorces, robberies, rapes, jail terms, bloody accidents, acts of the government in Washington, in Des Moines, and in the Linn County courthouse and in the mayor's office (my father suspected them all; he just wanted to be left alone to work like a dog without interference, even from actions supposed to be for his own good), advertisements for plumbers, clothing, shoes, shirts, socks, rugs, autos. In brief, the newspaper I threw onto the porch from my bicycle as I rode on the sidewalk contained not just "news" but human life in its entirety.

Before collecting our papers at the *Gazette* we would have a half hour or an hour to spend. In summer, we would walk along the riverbank behind an old hotel. Huge rats lived in the basement. Often we would see one scuttling along the cinders or even swimming in the river. Instead of everyone throwing stones at once, we agreed to throw one at a time, in order to know exactly who hit a rat. It didn't happen often; they were faster than our stones.

One winter a new bridge was being built from the east-bank end of 1st Avenue to the west bank. With a lot of time to kill, because it was Saturday and I had come earlier than on the days when I had to wait for school to end, I walked along a work area under the first arch. The dam was just above the bridge one block, so that the current was rapid, and although the river was frozen, there were holes in the ice. I slipped and fell. I had on heavy overcoat, boots, mittens, stocking cap. The flow of water carried me under the ice and downstream. Turning my face up to catch the thin layer of air above the water, I saw that the ice, which looked dark from above, was radiant white with the sunlight falling through it. To me, freezing to death as well as drowning, it was the colorless color of hope. The overcoat must have kept me from sinking, for the ice kept me from swimming, and besides, within seconds I was almost too numb to move. My canvas *Gazette* bag was slung over my left shoulder, filling with water and dragging me down, but it was my job, it belonged with me. I clung to it.

Suddenly my head bobbed up into the air at another hole in the ice. I took a long breath and yelled. On the bank were other newsboys, my friends. Lumber was scattered along the cinders, fallen from the frames and scaffolding of the bridge. They grabbed a plank and shoved it across the ice. I had hit the downstream edge of the hole and was about to go under again. Another immersion in that water which was like liquid ice and I would have been a body washing up on a sandbar in the spring.

As I was going under for certainly the last time the plank hit my head. Half aware, half alive, I threw my hands over it and hung on to that piece of dead wood as if it were my life. But it was!

Every motion of every muscle hurt, but I pulled my chest up on the plank. No farther. All of my body in the water was paralyzed, slipping back into the drag of the current. I couldn't even yell. But my fellow carrier boys could yell! They screamed at me to hang on, they grabbed the plank and pulled. I put my head on that hard board and gave up, for I could not move myself an inch. Then the plank crept a little over the ice. My waist began to leave the water. Another tug, and my *Gazette* bag crawled up and began to empty its weight of water. The ice under me cracked and trembled. I shook. When the freezing air hit my soaked body it seemed to burn.

Inch by tortured inch I was pulled out of the river and across the ice to the bank. I could not move, but the kids howled at me, "You can't stay here, Paul, you gotta get inside." They took my arms and legs and stood me up, swaying, unable to speak, the one word "warm" bouncing around in my brain like a heated marble. I took a step and stopped. It was ten below zero. That air froze my clothes solid, so that I could not walk inside a suit of ice. The kids grabbed me and carried me up the bank and into the pressroom where the furnaces for melting used lead forms (it was the old way of printing newspapers) were furiously hot with molten metal. They stretched me out on the floor. As soon as the ice melted from one garment they took it off and put it by the furnace to dry. When I was naked, they rubbed my skin, pounded it with the side of their hands, begged me to speak, as if I were a dog.

Without that pressroom I would have died. Without that hole, without that plank, without those carrier boys, I would have died. I looked death in the face — it was white as sunlight.

The afternoon edition began to roll. My blood began to roll. The kids lined up for their papers. My special friend, a Czech in my class at school (he played the violin), helped dress me, took my arm while I walked slowly around the pressroom. I tottered as if drunk, but gradually the shaking stopped. My overcoat, boots, mittens, stocking cap had dried rapidly in that intense heat, so that when I put them on they toasted my skin.

I got in line, filled my *Gazette* bag with my eighty papers. Everyone said, "Paul, go home and go to bed. Forget it today. They'll get somebody."

But I was a *Gazette* carrier boy. I had my job to do. I went, so that those friends waiting for me could have their evening news. Besides, my father had trained me for disasters. Almost drowning was like being thrown under a horse. His instructions for any bad scene were given me in expressive English: "Paul, it don't matter what happens. Just haul your ass up off the ground and get goin'." I got goin'.

Glowing with heated clothes, I walked through snow the long blocks from 1st Avenue and 1st Street SE to the corner of 4th Avenue and 15th Street SE, where my first delivery was the house on the northeast corner.

Never think that a paper route (we called it "rout") is dull. I loved that mile and a half of small wooden houses on a tree-lined Iowa street, trees that spread up and outward, meeting high above the middle of the street, so that walking along them in summer was going through a green tunnel. Those houses at a distance looked calm, quiet, outside the turbulent world. But to a boy of twelve they were crammed with excitement, with living, tense, often wild faces. Windows were the way I looked into their eyes.

There was a house that evening where I saw husband and wife, who had joked with me in the summer, screaming at each other in their dining room. She scooped up a handful of mashed potatoes and threw it in his face. (I could tell they were mashed by the sloppy way they spread over his nose and chin.) He slapped her so hard she fell over the chair and down on the floor. I was appalled and fascinated. It was fighting as tough as in Alex Fidler's boxing room. I knew that I was wrong to stay there and watch; I was ashamed to see their tragedy, but if it had to take place, I had to see it. It was a clean knockdown. Was she out for the count? Neither moved a muscle save their glaring eyes. Then he headed around the table toward her. What should I do? Would a man feel a duty to help her? Even a twelve-year-old boy, bent over with his heavy bag of papers, could be a nuisance to an adult, maybe slow him down a little. I took a few steps up the sidewalk for a closer look, ready to bang on the door if he beat her again. Then I saw that he too was weeping. Men didn't cry in our house, where the law, no matter how furious the emotion, was to tough it out.

She was too stunned to get up or even lift her arms.

He leaned over and kissed her.

The drab brown rug on which she lay, in that square box of a room with its ugly furniture, with food getting cold on the table, seemed to glow. I ran to the next house.

Over the years I saw them hundreds of times, looking happy enough together, but always behind them I saw the dark shadow of that quarrel.

The pressroom warmth had long gone from my clothes. I had become chilled standing there. I walked on up 4th Avenue, baffled by what I had seen, yet feeling that somehow I had been lucky, that it had been beautiful.

In another window three girls had joined hands and were dancing in a circle. In another a boy was teaching his dog to sit. He had a bone in his left hand and was holding it above his pet's head. A cat lay on the rug a few feet away watching the lesson with smug, contemptuous eyes. No human being, however arrogant, can express contempt and superiority like a well-fed cat.

In another window a man and a woman were facing each other. Tears were running down their cheeks. He reached over and slapped her shoulder. More fight, I assumed, and waited. Then I saw that those were tears of laughter. He touched her other shoulder with his other hand. It was the end of their working day, he was home from office or factory or store with a new joke (he was still talking, so it must have been his story).

I had a short street called Upland Drive, 4th Avenue ending for a couple of blocks. My first house belonged to a retired schoolteacher who took a great interest in my physical and mental well-being. On that day she met me at the door with hot milk and a piece of pecan pie, a delicacy I had never eaten before. "Come in and get warm, Paul," she called to me even before I could throw her *Gazette* on the porch. She had been waiting at the window. The first woman in my life to wait for me at a window, she was skinny, tall, nervous, and in love with food. And also, perhaps, with small Paul, for she always patted my head, and sometimes a cheek, when I came into her house for cake or cookie or pie, all the rich things on which she did not gain an ounce. When she retired, she crowded her little house with her library. Having spent forty years of school days dealing with the young, she was suddenly backed up against the wall of old age and of old people who bored her, as she told me: "Paul, when I was a teacher, I always felt young with the kids in my classes. Then one day they told me I was old and had to leave. Now I just see people my own age. Do you know something? I prefer kids. Even the mean ones are livelier than the old coots I see."

She gave me the complete poems of Henry Wadsworth Longfellow. (Why did those writers in the middle of the nineteenth century have three names—Henry David Thoreau, Ralph Waldo Emerson, Julia Ward Howe, James Fenimore Cooper, Harriet Beecher Stowe—when today two names—Robert Frost, Sinclair Lewis—are enough?) Almost every week she would take a book from a shelf and give it to me with the simple remark that still sounds like the best literary criticism I have heard, "Here, I read it. You read it." Warmed by the house, by the pie, by her care, by the book crouching in my canvas paper bag, I went on to my next short street, Meadowbrook Drive, then up to the final block of 4th Avenue.

At one house I always took the paper to the door and knocked, because the local poet, Jay Sigmund, lived there. By now I was shivering, weak, numb. With every *Gazette* I delivered, my paper bag became lighter, but with every step I took, I became feebler. When I knocked, Jay opened the door, only socks on his feet, a heavy man with a gift for the lightness of language. "Sit down, Paul. I'll read you a new poem." In a time of bone-bitter cold, he read the words of a bitter summer fisherman.

It's been a right tough spring,
The river's been too high;
The price of fish — oh, hell,
What good to cuss or cry . . .
I'm like a wing-tipped duck —
I'll never have no luck.

Jay moved slowly but his eyes moved fast. In the city he kept alive the rural life he knew as a boy along the Wapsipinicon River northeast of Cedar Rapids. He looked at me hard and said, "You look peaked." Then he quietly picked up another page of manuscript, without waiting for an answer, not wanting to probe the private life of anyone, not even an exhausted kid.

Indian Summer suns may blaze a trail
Over the smoky sky before the dusk;
The days are all alike as huddled quail —
The ripened corn is waiting in the husk.

In the business world where he spent his days, he made his practical way through actuarial tables, premiums, insurance policies, with poems hiding in his pockets like pups waiting to jump out and bark. For him the days were not "all alike as huddled quail." Each one was a new scrutiny of human faces, a sniff at the weather, a stare at the changing air, an ear for the babble of many voices on that round tower of Babel, the earth, rolling through space like an immense monosyllable "O."

Jay had grown up on a farm. He knew the sweat and strain of the body. "Paul, you better finish up and go home. You don't look good." Then he picked up a book, as he did on so many days when I stopped in. "Try this. I don't understand what in the hell he is doing, but some of it makes my hair curl." That was the greatest tribute, for Jay didn't have much hair, and all of it was straight.

He knew that I was writing what only I called poetry, most of it so bad it should have been piled in the barnyard along with that rich stuff whose smell itself was nourishing. The book contained T. S. Eliot's "Love Song of J. Alfred Prufrock." He opened the book and read me the opening lines: "Let us go then, you and I, / When the evening is spread out against the sky / Like a patient etherized upon a table . . ." I did not know whether T. S. Eliot had ever gone under the ice — he was a very secretive person, always going under something — but he knew how I felt, anaesthetized and stretched out. Later I read the whole poem and found that line which wrote my life on the paper route as I approached every house, pushing up my stocking cap, getting my smile ready, about how you "prepare a face to meet the faces that you meet." As I went out into the black and freezing air to the next house, the weight of books replacing the weight of papers, I prepared my face.

When my feet hit the porch steps, a dog inside began a deep-toned barking. It was Toby, an English bulldog, with a huge, savage jaw, tearing teeth, the shoulders of a defensive tackle, and a lust for being scratched just in front of his tail where no paw could reach. He knew my voice through the door and changed from a snarl to a whimper begging me to come in and scratch. There was a very old man in that house whom we knew simply as "the last survivor of the charge of the Light Brigade." He had ridden into that death trap as a young man, in a brilliant uniform of scarlet and other colors, swinging a saber reflecting the sun, mounted on a good horse and surely screaming whatever the English cavalry screamed in the Crimea to frighten the enemy. Now he was short and round, quick of step, with a deep voice that said to me every time I gave him his paper, "Great boy." Or was it, "Great, boy"? I believed in the first.

He was a gardener specializing in roses. Each summer he would give me cuttings from his bushes. I planted them in a row behind our house. The original roots had come from England, and I tended them with well-rotted manure, covering them in winter, not suspecting that in some years I would be living in a room at an English college overlooking a garden with what looked like those same roses. One above all I cherished, a red, red rose called, if I spell it properly, "Jacque-mont." (Was there a "Colonel" in front of it, my mind asks — but it was fifty-eight years ago, and time has stunned that memory a little, for I can recall the name of the flower but not the name of that ancient warrior.)

I pushed the paper in when he opened the door a crack, and he patted my hand and said "Great boy" or "Great, boy." I scratched Toby's spine just in front of his tail, refused an invitation to come in and get warm, and went on to my last place. I was so tired I had to think about moving one foot ahead of the other.

It was common on the edge of Cedar Rapids for people who could not afford a whole house to build a large garage and live in it a few years, until they could afford a real home. This meant very close living. Often the living room was also a bedroom. Because my last delivery was to such a garage, which had no porch where I could throw the paper, they had asked me to open the door a crack and shove it onto the floor. With hardly strength enough to turn the knob, I pushed the door open. A few feet away was a young and superbly crafted woman, stark naked.

I had never seen a fabulous feminine landscape before.

On that frozen, windy spot I had my first great moral dilemma. Should I slam the door and run away? It was a marvelous sight; could I not look a few seconds longer? (Thinking back, with the foolishness of years, I wonder if she might not have enjoyed my admiration.) Lust beat down fear. I stared. Then she said softly, with poise, her voice seeming to sing out of that beautiful body, "Thank you, Paul." Thanks for the paper? Thanks for closing the door? Thanks for watching her with wonder? All of it?

I turned away from that garage-home, freezing on the outside of my whole body yet burning inside, and began the long walk home. It was a brutal blackness I had to go through, few street lights, almost no cars, no one else out moving over the drifted snow. I felt myself growing numb as I pushed one foot in front of the other. Could I make it home?

Then abruptly the fear I had not felt in the river hit me. I began to shake, not only with cold, but with clean terror. I began to gasp, as if again under water. The wild wind out of the north seemed to blow not over the city but only on me. I stopped on that empty street and confronted the hopelessness of hope. My mind was darkening. If I stayed there, I knew I would die.

The street lights ahead were like dim stars in the night sky. Beyond them, a mile away, were the lights and warmth of our house, Mother keeping the kitchen alive with our simple food, Father reading the *Gazette* that another carrier had thrown on the porch, my sisters and brother reading, sewing, talking. I did what any sensible twelve-year-old boy facing dark death would always do. I ran. Staggered fast might be more accurate, for the total strain of that afternoon had taken away all my slender strength. Block after desperate block I staggered, until I reached our house. I do not remember opening the door, only throwing myself down on the sofa wearing stocking cap, overcoat, boots, mittens and crying, crying without words.

Mother held me until I calmed enough to tell her, "I fell in the river." Father came over, sniffed me, and as usual made the right remark: "You smell like catfish. Better get those clothes off." I could not undress. I could not eat. I could not talk. What they carried to bed was a stupefied body.

Two visions in one day are one too many. One was a vision of death as I sank in the killing water of the Cedar River, up to my mouth, my eyes watching white sunlight flaming through the air-bubbled ice. The other was a vision of life, electric light illuminating a woman's body like a living flame.

Always lead the visionary life. It is hell on the nerves, but you can warm your aching hands before a vision.

I was lucky to be a newsboy. When other kids my age were at home wasting their time (save one who took violin lessons, but he was regarded as eccentric), I was reading as well as delivering the news of the world, of Iowa, of Cedar Rapids, and earning seven dollars a month toward my college fund. I came to know many different sorts of life, Czech, black, Greek, Armenian kids from the working part of town, all the families along my route. Looking back, some might think my window observations were "peeping," but those were people I knew in all four seasons; their dogs, cats, and children were close to me. Why shouldn't I share in their grief, their joys, their modest wooden homes?

Some days the weight of books given me replaced the weight of the *Gazette* in my bag. I was educated out of that newspaper bag the way a horse is fed oats and corn out of its nose bag.

I was blessed by that sun pouring through the ice to reassure me. I was blessed by the radiance of that woman's skin. I was blessed, years later, by that poet Edmund Blunden, who had seen in battle a vision of hell on earth. I was blessed by that old, gentle fighter from England who shared his roses. In a poem about roses and poppies at Vlamertinghe in Flanders, Blunden hinted at the color of blood he had seen pouring out of the brutalized bodies of young soldiers.

> But if you ask me, mate, the choice of colour
> Is scarcely right; this red should have been duller.

Some people smoke pot, some get drunk, some overeat; I read newspapers, a morning, an afternoon, the *Des Moines Register*, the *Cedar Rapids Gazette*, the University of Iowa *Daily Iowan*, and the *New York Times*. I can get as immersed in stories about a small-town divorce, an accident on a country road, obituaries, farm problems, a new highway, or a new business, as I can in the great cataclysms of the great world. They are all human life.

For me as a child, selling and delivering newspapers was an intense and often fiery career. I was proud of it. I am still proud of it.

The Importance of Uncles

athers have a certain value. Without them there would not be that wild moment when a child begins those first floating months of his life inside his mother. Those will be the only untroubled months of his life. After he exchanges the safe liquid of the womb for the unstable air of the earth, all hell will break loose.

But uncles have their own marvelous powers. Not living in the boy's house, they have not heard the little varmint sassing his father or the howls when the temperature on his bottom was raised fifty degrees by his father's hot and hard hand. They did not see him hypocritically patting the family cat before pulling its tail, nor hear his whining excuses for not mowing the lawn or weeding the garden or raking the leaves. They never saw him sneaking off to the woods beyond the edge of town to look for butterfly cocoons, for slender mushrooms, for the rare pileated woodpecker, for the quick eyes of a raccoon circled in black. They did not know he stayed out until after dark while his mother waited in fear.

Father is day-by-day. Uncles are now-and-then. They see a boy only on visits when he is trying to behave better than his true nature. They bring him advice out of lives very different from his father's. A visit is a holiday, so that uncles are more cheerful than at home. They have loose change burning a hole in their pocket, sending a kid to the drugstore to buy cigars. (Once I got the Antonio y Cleopatra box because I bought the last three cigars; Cleopatra's scanty clothing indicated she came from a very hot country where a woman had to expose most of her skin to the soft air.) There would be a few pennies left, and as I held them out an uncle would say, "Keep 'em, Paul. And don't give 'em at Sunday School. Spend 'em, kid, spend 'em!" So they burned a hole in *my* pocket until I rushed back to the store and blew them on candy. Thus, I learned early a contempt for money and the joy of reckless spending.

Uncles were good to have. They were like fathers who didn't have to be responsible for you. It was far more man-to-man than son-to-father. Uncles could tell you things no one in the family would ever discuss. Down 5th Avenue there was a boy my age who had no uncles. He was the most deprived kid on the block and used to come to our house just to sit close and watch the respect and warmth with which those grown men treated young boys. He felt, as I did, the strength flowing from their big frames into our skinny ones. Some of my uncles had their own sons, but they were easier with me, because I was not underfoot all the time, and they always went home at night so that they did not have to see my beady but cheerful eyes staring at them first thing in the morning. My father trained saddle horses, my uncles raised purebred Jersey cattle, farmed in the stony acres of Minnesota, fished and made candy in Idaho, ran a brawny blacksmith shop with fire, steel horses, and curses, drove trotters and pacers in Iowa. How could a boy at the beginning of this mechanized century be so lucky as to have one real father and four half-fathers, all of whom worked with animals all their lives? They talked to me about how to handle those creatures, great or small, how to predict their actions a split second before they happened by watching for the faintest tensing of a muscle, a twitch of the head, a flick of tail or fin.

I learned to watch my uncles in the same way, alert to the lifting of a finger, the flicker of an eyelid, the shifting of a foot, or the clearing of a throat, which meant a sudden tough comment on a neighbor, an anecdote about a horse, dog, or cat, a quick joke. We were all animals who spoke English.

Uncleless days were like meatless days, less nourishing to a boy, less dramatic.

UNCLE GEORGE

Uncle George arrived with whistle, smoke, and steam at the Cedar Rapids railroad station on the Union Pacific train from Pocatello, Idaho. With his buffalo robe coat (he always came in winter), matching long mittens, and round buffalo hat, he brought the wild west into our quiet town. The engine pulled in, iron brake shoes grinding, steam hissing from hoses, the fireman shoveling coal into the flaming firebox, black smoke beating into the black night from the smokestack, brass bell clanging, the air still ringing with the deep whistle the engineer had given as he crossed the Cedar River bridge and headed for the station. It was a powerful sound, threatening, warning, announcing the arrival of iron power and traveling people.

Uncle George was the romantic in the Reinheimer family. He had been born on the little family farm near Marion where my mother, Uncle Charlie, and Aunt Lydia had also arrived, not in a hospital, but in that little, thin-walled, narrow house, freezing in winter, boiling in summer, in that marvelous, human, long-gone way—birth on the bed where the child had been conceived, a beautiful thing, a family matter with the kids standing outside the room, scared but excited, waiting for the first tiny howl which meant a new sister or brother. The thrust of the father's body was still on the sheet where the little creature lay, after its non-antiseptic, nondrug, wholly natural, wholly painful delivery (wonderful word, as if what was being delivered was not a living child but a sack of groceries— which, on that poor sandy farm, would also have been welcome). Did it give the newborn child a sense of security (that desperate, uncertain, twentieth-century word) which our antiseptic, impersonal world of the maternity ward cannot give?

Uncle George brought with him the high air of Idaho mountains, the furious presence of the Snake and Bannock Indians with whom he traded, the look of an unfenced landscape, the tang of sagebrush, the slither of trout in cold streams where you could see them hanging above the pebbled bottom that was as speckled as the fish. He was the only uncle who had left the Midwest. He had learned ice-cream and candy making in Cedar Rapids as a young man after deciding that farm life was not for him. Instead of milking cows, he converted milk into many-flavored ice cream and into chocolates cunningly molded into many shapes with fruit and nuts at their center (no, what a dull word, "center," it should be "at their heart," so cherished were they by us kids).

Plowing was too tedious, so George went west in that great flow of men and women from eastern cities and midwestern farms. He traveled for nights and days, sitting up in a scratchy green seat all the way, coal soot in his eyes.

The family legend is that when Uncle George arrived in Pocatello, he walked out of his bone-aching coach car, went back to a cattle car at the end of the train, saddled up his handsome chestnut horse, and rode into the city in style. There he opened an ice-cream and candy store with soda fountain, greeting card counter, and "sundries." Every few years he visited us in Iowa, and every year in December he sent a big box of candy. He began trading chocolates for beaded moccasins with Indians on the Snake River Reservation near Pocatello. We waited for "Uncle George's box" every Christmas. Would it arrive before the 25th? Would there be a new candy he had just invented? Above all, would there be deerskin moccasins on top of the box for the children? Each day after December 15 we waited for the card from American Express saying that there was a package waiting for the Engle family. Even Father was excited; he would leave the horse barn half-shoveled of its manure, throw a few ears of corn into the feed boxes so that the horses would not get so hungry they would stamp the planks on the stall floors — a steel-shod horse hoof can tear the hell out of even a tough piece of wood — come to the house to pick up all of us, and head down 5th Avenue to the Express office. In the early years he drove a big bobsled with its heavy runners and its wide bed covered with fresh straw. Bells on leather belts circled the horses, and as their backs moved up and down the bells were in steady motion, musically telling the world that the Engle family was on its way to get its wild-west candy.

I would do the dangerous thing by standing on a runner, hanging on to the side of the bobsled, where my feet trembled with the constant scraping of the runner over the rough ice and snow. That is the way to travel, feet a part of the moving steel snarling back at the unmoving ice.

At the American Express office, our box would be sitting on the floor, wrapped in heavy brown paper like dozens of other packages headed for lucky homes. Yet for us it had a radiance around it a little like the light in that faraway desert manger where the Child whose birthday we were celebrating had been born, for our box too was magical.

Father carried it out to the bobsled, and because we could not wait to open it, he kept the horse at a fast trot home. Mother sat closest to the box, crouching in the straw with one hand firmly on it (she was gentle but strong), now and then patting it with her hand as if it were a child. For months we had known the box was coming. Then suddenly it was there, sitting in straw from a barn, after its long journey over mountains, through deep valleys, along trout streams, across the high western plains deep in snow, down to our rolling Iowa prairie country shaped into square fields bearing corn, oats, alfalfa, and timothy hay, with fat beef animals nosing under the snow for dropped ears of corn. We stared at that box with hunger, reverence, and pride, for no other kids in our neighborhood had such an uncle living in such wild country and sending such a gift of sweet things at Christmas. What a wise man Uncle George was.

At home, Father would tie the horse to the hitching post, throw a warm blanket over its back, muffling the still clanging, ringing bells, and carry the box into the house as if it were a sleeping child. He would cut the heavy cords around it, but then the youngest child was allowed to open it. I had that daring and delicate job until my younger sister Kathryn came along. She was the last to open the Idaho treasures, until they stopped coming when George died.

Kathryn carefully removed the swaddling paper, not throwing it wildly away in a heap but smoothing it out and then folding it into a neat rectangle. It had protected a long-awaited and cherished gift at a holy time. A moment of respectful silence before Kathryn with her small hands gave us the moment of revelation by lifting the four cardboard flaps of the top. The exciting years were those when the first objects we saw were Snake Indian moccasins with their intricate designs worked out in many-colored beads. We smelled that deerskin, we stroked it, we caressed it with our eyes, we imagined the browsing, brown animal lightly lifting its feet in a wild western valley. Now its hide was held in our hands. We also saw the brown hands of the Indian women stitching the soft but tough leather. Indian men had killed the deer with their hands. That trading event was handmade, for George had rolled and dipped and dripped with his own hands the chocolates that he brought to the reservation and exchanged for the moccasins. It was the old American manner — you gave to someone what you had made with your hands for what he or she had made with equally skilled hands.

Next was always a fancy box tied with a red ribbon and a big bow. On the lid was the portrait of a woman, dressed (undressed!) in a way that proved that the candy in the box was of such a delicacy that you could not eat it wearing all your clothes but had to strip down to bare skin. The proportions of the lady also hinted that eating those chocolates produced breasts of remarkable size and fullness. Indeed, that was the closest I had ever come to a naked bosom. (This flaw in my character was later corrected.)

At this point there was always a debate, along age lines, between the parents and older child on one side and the three younger children on the other. Should the special box be opened at once or put aside for a more ceremonial occasion like Christmas Eve, when it would become a part of the whole celebration rather than an object of our instant lust for chocolate? Usually, it was reluctantly put aside while the next layer was revealed, quite enough in itself to satisfy our animal appetite, for it was always rolls of pecans around a rich, thick center. Nibbling at that was allowed. The next layer was of George's huge mystery chocolates, five times the size of an ordinary piece, with the filling densely flavored with maple and a strange, musky, irresistible taste we could not identify. Aunt

Tillie, who always came for the opening, loved that strange and exotic candy above all others. She would bite out a little piece of the outer layer, then hold the chocolate to her nose and deeply inhale the odor of the filling. Tillie was a rabid Prohibitionist. Many years later I visited Pocatello and found George's closest friend, who had worked for him in the store. He wrote down the secret formula for that filling. The magic ingredient, which George never revealed, was rum. So Tillie sat there shouting about the evils of strong drink while inhaling the beautiful scent of old rum.

In the bottom of the box was a deep layer of peanut (and sometimes, rarely, almond) brittle, often with a few perfectly chipped arrowheads, of the kind that might have destroyed the deer that gave us our moccasins.

Uncle George was like all the Reinheimers, kind, thoughtful, generous, too easygoing to succeed in a competitive world. He was also the only uncle to give up the tough and often violent world of farm and horse for the indoor life of the city. When he and the other uncles returned for a family reunion, usually at Christmas, we always shook hands. Uncle Herman from the north Minnesota farm, Uncle Billie from the racetrack, and Uncle Charlie from the Iowa dairy farm all had hard calluses on the palms of their hands, but Uncle George's skin was soft. Yet his grip was firm on my small fingers; he kept active by walking miles in the mountains and fishing the streams flowing out of them, whose water temperature varied from very cold to unbearably cold. George was also the only bachelor among them. The other uncles and my father regarded him with a very slight pity because he had no family, and with a certain envy for his freedom to go where he wished (and with *whom* he wished; there were rumors, largely from Aunt Tillie, that George "was no better than he ought to be," and was, in fact, worse than he ought to be). I used to sniff him for lingering odors of perfume rubbed off from the sort of women one uncle described, with contempt and admiration, as "friendly." At ten years, I found all women friendly. Later?

George had one particular friend who turned up in Iowa to

meet the family, a voluptuous creature round in all the parts I was able to see. George was a handsome man with strong bones, like all the Reinheimers, especially in the face. She was indeed friendly. I was ill and lying on the couch in our living room when she came in and said, "Paul, I've heard about you." Her presence caressed the air above me. I had a fever of a hundred and two. I felt it rising. It turned out that she was less interested in the bad health of George's nephew than in the good value of his share in the family farm. She departed disillusioned.

George laughed a lot, and he always spent a lot of time with me because he had no kids of his own. One day, when I was twelve and growing fast, I was scratching my crotch because I had a pair of rough, new, unfinished worsted trousers (we always called them "pants"). George looked over and said, "What's your problem, Paul, too many women?" He winked at me, man to man.

While lecturing in the northwestern states I found that, by taking an extra couple of days between talks, I could go through Pocatello. All I had was the name of a man who had been with George. I found him in the phone book, and we met within an hour. He was tall and husky, uneducated but quick of mind, open to all questions, just the sort of man George would have wanted to know. When he gave me the secret recipe for the rum chocolates, he said, "By God, I miss 'em myself." He drove me into the Porte Neuf mountains to the narrow, fast, deep, transparent river where George had cast for trout with him. We parked by a bridge.

He said, "Look upstream. George and I came here and decided he would go above the bridge to fish and I would go below the bridge. I went down for an hour, caught three beauties and was casting for another when I saw George coming down the river under the bridge.

"There he was, by God, floating down the river, standing up because his waders had filled with water, dead."

Then he pointed to a high rock. "I was over there and so damn surprised George went right on by before I realized he couldn't talk when I yelled at him. Must have had a heart attack and fallen into the river. He looked just like he was tryin' to find a better fishing place. So I had to run down the bank a ways until he came close enough so I could grab his collar. Heavy, with all that water. I dragged him up to the bridge and stuffed him in the backseat of the car. Then I went upstream where he'd been and found his string of trout and his pole. George loved that pole, he wouldn't've wanted it left there."

A silence, while he looked up at the snowy range, and then he added, "If he'd known you were coming, he'd have wanted you to have it."

We drove back to look at the building where George had run his candy and ice-cream store. It had glittered in my mind as a boy, that great place from which the Christmas candy came. It was a drugstore, small, badly lit.

When I flew out of the Pocatello airport the next day, I looked up at the Porte Neuf mountains to the gap where the river of the same name roared down with its melted snow. Like my father falling dead from his saddle on his favorite horse, George died doing what he most enjoyed, up in the high air, casting into a pool for the quick trout whose flesh was firm in the cold water (it turned pink when cooked). What a way to go— held upright by the fast water he loved, a man floating out of the mountains where he had spent most of his life, strong arms with hands delicate at rolling chocolates and flicking a fly rod.

I flew over the Union Pacific railroad tracks that had carried the Christmas box to farming Iowa because childless George thought of those faraway nieces and nephews whom he seldom saw. The Reinheimers were like that.

UNCLE HERMAN

We always called him Herm, Father's brother, the one with the greatest amount of Engle reticence, the quietest of the brothers. All his life he farmed, starting on a small place north of Cedar Rapids. He was heavier than the others, thick shoulders and arms, calluses on his hands like shoe leather. We used to hitch up the surrey (with a fringe around the top and a holder for the buggy whip by the front seat) and drive to Herm's acres, one of those general farms which raised a little of everything, but not enough of any one thing to make money. Compared to an all-grain, all-hog, or all-beef operation, it was full of excitement for a child. There were pigs swilling and swearing in their barn, a few Guernsey dairy cattle, a flock of Rhode Island Reds with the burnished rooster strutting around making promises to his hens which, if made by a man to women, would have been actionable at law. "Paul, get yourself a really fresh egg," Herm would say, and I would go into the hen house to search. The best moment was when one of the hens, startled by my sudden appearance, would cluck and mumble and cuss as she abandoned the nest. I picked up an egg still warm from her body, rolling it in my hands to get the hard smoothness of the shell. So warm, so smooth, it seemed alive in my hands.

There was a flock of white sheep on the farm, with a curl-horned ram. Herm had some tame pigeons, and he had trained one to ride on the ram's back and trained the ram (when it was very young) to accept it. One day the ram came around a corner with an iridescent pigeon clinging to the wool of its back, rolling its head and cooing its joy in pigeon. "Well, Paul," Herm said, "if a little bird can ride that buck, a big boy like you can." I wasn't a big boy; I was a skinny kid of seven. The only strength I had was in my will power and in my stupidity in never refusing a dare. And in my gut reaction to failure. I had ridden ponies — which could be tough and mean — both saddled and bareback, at my father's barn. I sidled up to Billy on the left side, facing his rear, as Father had beaten into me, grabbed the thick white mane above his shoulders, and swung up onto his back. The blue-rose-gray-feathered pigeon hopped up between the horns, sneering and swearing softly. A horse would have bucked, but Billy took off running, swerving from side to side, cutting in tight circles, bleating in outraged buck language (translated, his remarks would have been unprintable in English). I dug my hands deeper in the wool; the pigeon did the same with its feet while muttering sounds such as I had heard only once before in my life, when my vigorously unmarried Aunt Jane, a fighting Christian sworn not to swear, muttered and crooned in pain when she stabbed her finger doing a doily. I was shocked at her wordless outburst. It was harsher than profanity.

Uncle Herm was howling, "Hang on, Paul. Ride 'im, cowboy." My sisters watched, silent, mouths open, appalled. A mouth open and screaming is fine; I needed noisy support, but a mouth open and silent is frightening.

Mother came out the back door of the little farmhouse, saw the disaster, and threw her apron up over her face.

Father relit his strong cigar, a Harvester (he never smoked a cigar not named after a horse, although he was tempted by the undraped figure of Cleopatra on the inside lid of the Antonio y Cleopatra box), spat a bit of tobacco leaf on the barnyard, yelled "Damn fool" at me, and blew smoke rings into the compassionate air.

"Hey, Uncle Herm," I yelled, "get me off." Judging by its hysterical mumblings (can a mumble be hysterical?), the pigeon also thought that was a great idea. Chickens and turkeys ran away with a shrill squawking and a dropping of fear-loosened tail feathers. Cows and a couple of horses watched happily over the pasture fence; there wasn't a lot of vaudeville in their lives. Their jaws happily rolled a cud of grass over tongues, and green saliva drooled from their mouths.

Billy kept going at top speed, heading straight for the fence. Within inches of it he dug his hooves deep into the soft barnyard dirt and stopped. Pigeon and Paul flew through the air, the bird on wings, Paul on his tense and frightened belly. If he had hit the top strand of the barbed-wire fence, it would have taken off his head. The pigeon, cussing and cooing, sailed up the corncrib and perched on the roof, fluttering its wings, stamping up and down on its delicate pink feet. I hit the ground so hard it knocked my breath out and brought blinding suns into my eyes.

Billy bleated and swore, jumped up and down stiff-legged,

pawed the ground, shook his horns like a mad bull, then trotted around in circles, celebrating his victory over that beastly boy.

Lying in the cow manure–covered grass of the pasture, I heard my father's voice: "Serves the fool right. By God, I'll teach him to ride." And by God, he did. Herm yelled, "You need help, Paul?" My mother yelled to everyone in range of her voice (she was a farm girl used to calling pigs and cattle; her voice traveled far), "Somebody pick him up, maybe he's hurt."

I began to breathe again, sat up, and saw my ultimate humiliation. The pigeon flew on its blue-rose-gray-feathered wings over the barnyard and dropped between Billy's horns. Together they circled that ram-glorious, pigeon-proud, kid-cruel yard. I could have gone back to Uncle Herm's farmhouse, washed my hands and face, and forced down a plate of turnip greens with ham, but I would have seen all those faces, however friendly, staring at a defeated boy, their son, their cousin, their nephew, beaten to the ground by a sheep and a bird. Had those animals planned it that way? Did they talk it over? Could ram coo and pigeon bleat, or did they share barnyard English picked up from Uncle Herm? Stinking from the several sorts of manure in which I had rolled, still scared, still shaking, still ashamed, I looked once at all those people on the back porch and ran for the timber. There was a sandy creek flowing through it and I rolled in it, clothes on, to clean my body, my shirt, my overalls, and my mind.

All afternoon I walked through the hickory and oak trees. No one came from the house. People with a poor country-school education, and some with less, had the delicate instinct to let a terrified and humiliated kid make his own peace in the wilderness.

Toward supper time and after the milking, I heard Uncle Herm calling my name, then saw his short and powerful body pushing through the hazel brush under the trees, a hard man speaking my name softly. When he reached me he patted my shoulder and praised me: "By God, Paul, you did a damn fine job. Never thought you'd hang on that long. He's a tough one, Billy. Don't think I could ride 'im."

Uncle Herm the silent, don't-show-emotion man, like all the Engles, the farmer whom I had seen, pitchfork in hand, stare down a bitter bull, led me through that green and high-branched grove as if I were a champion. I had climbed up those black walnut trees to shake down the sweet-flavored, stone-hard nuts for Aunt Rose's Christmas cake. Through Uncle Herm's strong gesture, I had won victory over my weakness. His hands had calluses rough as walnut bark.

Herm's farm was fifteen miles north of Cedar Rapids and had good dirt (even the roads were good dirt: you could have planted them and had a fine crop of corn), but it was small. He sold it for a far larger farm in northwest Minnesota, his judgment being in favor of acres. We visited him there one summer, driving in an old Dodge with cloth top and awkward side curtains for rain, a "touring" car my father had bought by selling gaited saddle horses for all of that stinking horsepower. (Put the smell of horse manure alongside the odor of gasoline fumes; no problem deciding which is the more beautiful.) The roads on the way to his farm were sand and gravel from old glaciers; after a rain, they were still solid. In Iowa following a rain, you couldn't drive without sinking hub-deep. The farm was poor: some fields of flax raised for seed, blue flowers wavering like water in the northern breeze, a cornfield stubby, pale, and thin by Iowa standards, with little ears we called "nubbins," a big vegetable garden with poorly growing plants, a barn with work horses, a few thin pigs and cows, and a lot of pine trees, not worth an acre of that black Iowa soil Herman had left behind. There was also a lot of tamarack swamp, dense, full of wild animals. I was told never to go there.

The reason was wolves (more likely coyotes, I know now). I sneaked a little way into the tamarack one day and disappeared from the world. It was dark, the air still, although I could hear the wind shuffling through the top of the jack pines. After five minutes, I could not tell where I had entered, where the house was. The living trees were only two feet across, but under them were stumps three and four feet across, left from the original cutting of the first forest. Some stumps were five or six feet across. But where was home? From one direction I heard snuffling, muffled barks that could not have come from dogs. Birds were making threats and songs in the trees. Could those animals be between me and the farmhouse? I didn't have the guts to run toward them, so I turned and stumbled, groped, fought the opposite way, the bushes brushing tears from my eyes, which were already crying from fright. Suddenly I broke out into the lane leading from the county road to the farm and ran in marvelous sunlight toward Uncle Herm, who was walking from the barn after milking and feeding his cows.

"Fastest I ever saw you move, Paul," he laughed. "Got a bee in your britches?"

I told him about the sounds in the swamp.

"Paul, you're a nice boy but you're a durn fool," Herm said. "Lemme tell you about last winter. I'd gone to New York Mills in the bobsled. On the way home, a pack of wolves came out of the tamarack and started hacking and howling at the horses. If one of the team went down, if they could hamstring just one, we'd've all been goners. I didn't have to yell at the horses. They could smell those wolves, and they could see them closing in. Those horses took off like their ass was on fire, but the wolves stayed with us. That time I was a durn fool too, I didn't take my rifle with me to town."

But he did have a long whip with a snapper on the end. When a wolf got in position to bite at a horse leg, Herm snapped the whip past its ear with a crack like a pistol shot. That went on for two miles, the wolves tearing the air with their snow-white teeth and yelling together, the horses gulping the frozen air in and gasping hot air out, but pulling the bobsled fast, Herm cracking his whip from side to side and sometimes catching a wolf right on the ear and tearing it a little, so that the animal cried so loud the other wolves slowed up a little.

When Herm came to the place where his farm lane left the county road, he began to shout for Aunt Rose, his wife, without stopping the bullet-sounding whip. The wolves jumped in nearer, sensing the human house ahead.

Rose was an abundant, cheerful, round, strong woman who prayed every day and as a Seventh-Day Adventist observed Saturday as the Sabbath. She ran out in the yard, brought Herm's rifle up to her shoulder, and began firing. The first shot hit a steel runner and threw off sparks. The wolves veered away from the horses, giving Rose a clearer chance. She shot the lead wolf in the shoulder, and he went down howling. Another she got in the hindquarters, another in the head. They all rolled in the reddening snow, biting at the wounds. By now they were within a hundred feet of the house, and the last two wolves ran raving into the swamp. Rose grabbed the terrified horses, which were sweating as if it were a burning August day. Herm took the rifle and some cartridges from her, went back down the lane, finished off the wounded wolves, and headed into the tamarack. Rose told me she walked the team to the barn, unharnessed and blanketed them, then waited, watched, worried. "That swamp's no place for nobody," she told me. The afternoon darkened, and the wide woods were so silent that, Rose said, "you could hear snowflakes banging into each other."

Then a shot. A long wait. Rose headed for the swamp, bare-handed. She was Herm's wife.

A second shot. Rose kept on going. Then Herm came slowly out of the woods, dragging a dead wolf over the other bodies in the lane.

"Come on," Rose said, "I'll fix some supper."

"One more wolf," Herm told her, and went back into the black swamp while she held the rifle. Now it was night. The snow blackened, the stars brightened over a small farm wrangled by strong arms and a believing woman out of wilderness.

Herm staggered out of the swamp with the fifth wolf and laid it by the other bodies. Next morning he loaded them in the bobsled and hung them up outside the barn. Then he had his photo taken with an old box Brownie, standing by them, arms folded over his chest, legs apart, staring at the camera as he had stared into the menace of the swamp, proud to show that the wolves were two feet longer from muzzle to tail than he was. The rifle leans against the biggest wolf. That photo howls, cracks, yells.

One morning Herm came to my room and shook me awake. He was the sturdiest of the Engle brothers. His physical force was so great, he seemed six inches taller than he really was. My father, Tom, and Uncle Billie were like most horsemen, slender, wiry, tough. When Herm shook me, the bed shook. He put a finger over his mouth and jerked his head toward the barn. Pulling on my pants and shoes, I sneaked after him down the stairs to the front door. The sun was pouring its thick horizon gold on the barnyard, where several deer were nibbling hay along with the cattle.

"They come every morning," Herm told me, "so I throw out a little extra hay at night."

Like all Engle men, Herm never showed emotion publicly, save at the harsh crises of birth, death, or unbearable pain. His fields were poor glacial sands, producing a thin crop of hay, hardly enough to get his cows through the winter. He had given up a little Iowa farm with rich soil for a big farm of sand, swamp, trees. But he shared.

Sensing us, the deer ran across the yard, leapt the fence like brown light, and fled into the swamp.

One day Herm said, "We're goin' fishing tomorrow. That Big Pine Lake is full of perch and pike and pickerel and bass and trout, and anybody but a durn fool can catch 'em." ("Durn" was the most violent cuss word he could say in the presence of his abundant, kind, religious wife, Rose, as it was with Uncle George and Uncle Charlie. My father and Uncle Billie used the common form — and worse.)

Next day we packed into the big farm wagon, the bed covered with shiny oat straw, and Herm drove his team of bays down the gravel road through pine forests so strange to us kids from the elm-oak-maple-hickory-black-walnut woods of Iowa. I kept an eye out for wolves, but Herm said they didn't come out in summer. "How about a bear?" I asked. Herm looked at me grimly and pointed with his whip. "Saw one just about there last summer," he muttered. "Maybe we ought to get out of here." He touched the rumps of the team with the snapper on his whip and took them along the road at a heavy trot, glowering into the woods and then at me. No bear.

At Big Pine Lake we got two rowboats and some minnows for bait. I was in the boat Herm rowed. I had a long pine branch stripped of its twigs for a pole, a line with hook and lead sinker at the end. "Drop 'er about five feet," Herm said, "and don't let any whales pull you out of the boat."

We had left the Iowa August air, sultry and damp, dusty, corn pollen thick in the nose, the lifting of an arm causing sweat. Now the Minnesota breeze brought the tang of lake water, pine trees, coolness, a scent of fish (ripe from the dead washed up on the beaches), and no dust at all, for it was glacial sand, not fit to make dust like the black loam of Iowa). Herm rowed out a ways and said, "Now just about here there's a ledge about eight feet down. Fish feed along it."

Herm took a live minnow and put my hook through its back so that it could still make swimming movements. I didn't have the nerve to do it myself, but his thick fingers made one quick twist and threw hook and sinker into the lake.

We trolled slowly. "Now remember," Herm said, "when you feel a nibble on the line, don't pull up. Wait a few seconds, and then jerk the hook to set it."

Over in a weedy bay bass were jumping. The pine forest was so dark a green it seemed black between the tree trunks; I thought of the wolves in there, the rare bear, the dappled deer. It was a wilderness life I was leading, away from the tamed woods of Iowa and the hot street corner in Cedar Rapids where I shouted the *Gazette* headlines.

My line twitched; little ripples ran out in circles. A live creature was down there, connected to my hands by a piece of string. I jerked the hook, the line went taut, and Herm shouted, "Pull easy, keep the line tight." The line went in circles as the fish swam down in the deep water. Slowly I reeled in, my hands shaking. Slowly a silver-gleaming perch rose, fighting my hands. There was the first fish of my life. Herm said, "We'll have 'im for supper, Paul. You're a real fisherman."

Then under the perch there was a swirl in the water, and a four-foot-long dark fish appeared. As it rose toward the perch I could see that it was speckled, thin for its length, with a mouth full of teeth. "That's a pickerel," Herm yelled. Herm was always a calm man, but now he was excited and leaning out of the boat. I kept on pulling and almost had my fish in the boat when the pickerel lunged up and grabbed it.

"Hang on," Herm shouted. "Don't pull. Lemme get the net under that lunker."

As he spoke, I jerked the line in my inexperience and excitement. Minnow, perch, and pickerel jumped out of the water and swam in the air and the sunlight, glittering, live, twisting. Placid Aunt Rose was screaming. Herm said, his voice now soft, reassuring, talking to me the way my father talked to an overexcited horse, "Easy, Paul, easy, easy." He spoke the words rhythmically, songlike, as men comfort animals.

The underbelly of the pickerel was gray-white; the speckles along his sides gleamed in the sudden light. He (she? how does one tell on a pickerel?) swam and danced.

The pickerel made no sound, but I could tell by his furious eyes (were they a mad green?) at the level of my own blue eyes that he was swearing inside with revolting words in fish language.

The pickerel gave a great twisting lunge, clamped his jaws on the perch, which had already bitten the minnow, sailed through the air, perch in mouth, and dove into the lake. For a moment we saw him swimming violently down in the clear water, becoming a shadow and then disappearing.

I reeled in my half minnow. And wept.

Tough old Herm, whom I had seen carrying hundred-pound boulders across a field, took two steps to me in the rocking rowboat and patted my shoulder. "By God, Paul, you showed those fish. Best action I ever saw on this lake. You're a natural-born fisherman. Now there's a place I know where pike hang out, big ones, hungry. Lemme put a fresh minnow on your hook."

He rowed a quarter of a mile, and we dropped our lines

from opposite ends of the boat, but I could hardly see my line touch the water for the tears. I wanted to get ashore, walk into the scary pine forest, and be eaten by bears. Or run with the delicate-hooved deer until I dropped. Or find a sullen skunk to spray me until I stank so revoltingly that I could never go back to Herm's farm or to my forgiving family. Or crawl down a groundhog burrow and crouch in the comforting dark, where no one could see my shame. Or creep under pine needles and starve, so that a hundred years later the *Minneapolis Star* could report that "the skeleton of a boy aged about eight was recently found near Big Pine Lake, well-preserved, probably Indian."

"Hey, Paul," Herm yelled, "look at your line." It was swirling, not in circles but back and forth, which Herm said meant that a fish was examining it but had not taken the minnow. Then the line straightened, and Herm said quietly, "He's got the hook in his mouth. Jerk."

I jerked, the line moved sideways, and Herm came to my end of the boat. "You've got 'im, Paul. The way your rod is bending I'd say there's about four to five pounds down there. Now reel in slow, let 'im have time to get tired." I played the fish. The fish played me, swimming in circles, then cutting across in a straight line, then off on a wavering course. But all the time I slowly reeled it in until it was visible — a fighting, fine, solid pike, with its meat made firm and delicate by the cold water.

"There's our dinner," Herm told me, "if you just keep the pressure on and don't let 'im shake the hook."

I kept reeling. Herm took the dip net when the pike was within a foot of the surface, and with a quick swing of his arm, a long curve of the net through the air, into the water, up through the air, he landed the fish in the bottom of the boat, wriggling, defending its life.

As we drove up the farm lane from the sandy road I saw the little white farmhouse, the red barn, the brown deer leaping the fence where they had been browsing on hay the cattle had not eaten, the intense green pine trees, the blue flax fluttering in the wind, the gray glacial rocks, ten feet high, rolled out of Canada, along the edge of the woods. Herm had brought his wolves up that lane. I brought my pike.

Herm had sold his small Iowa farm because in northwestern Minnesota he could have four times as much land. He was a moving-on American. *Far away* was the place to live. *Here* was the place to leave. So he got his big farm in the big woods. He and Rose and the girls led a grinding, rocky life: cut thin hay on thin soil, plant potatoes in the sandy field. Herm once made one of his few jokes to me. "Paul, when we dig potatoes, we take along a hammer with the spade. If we think it's a potato, we tap it. If it cracks, it's a potato. If it doesn't, it's a stone."

That night I walked in my sleep. Aunt Rose took my arm before I fell down the stairway. "They got away," I told her. "The fish got away."

"Not the pike," Aunt Rose whispered. (The house was dark; people were sleeping all around us.) Herm carried me back to bed. The calluses on his hands scratched my skin.

UNCLE CHARLIE

Charlie had all the warm, kind qualities of the Reinheimers along with a soft heart, a farmer's hard hands, a wrestler's shoulders, and long brown curls. He was of medium height, liked having people around, and loved to talk; when he was alone he talked to the purebred Jersey dairy cattle he raised. He was closest to a hero in my childhood. At county fairs, where he exhibited his best cows and his bull and won many ribbons, there was a professional wrestler known as the Strangler, who would sit in his wrestling tights and robe on a platform with a ring mounted on it, challenging all comers. Anyone who could stay five minutes with him received fifty dollars, a golden sum in the early twentieth century. Most of the time his money was safe because he moved so fast the average country wrestler couldn't get a hold on him, but Charlie once went four minutes with him and then was put into a "hammer lock," the Strangler twisting Charlie's arm up behind his back and hanging on to the end. The greatest remark about me in my life was made by a neighborhood kid with whom I used to wrestle: "Paul's uncle stayed five minutes with the Strangler."

I strutted. I leered. I threatened. I intimidated. Until I took on a bigger kid, who threw me to the ground and put me in a hammer lock until I howled.

Let us now praise famous cows. The Jersey breed is often fawn-colored, yellow, brown, cream, and gentle, its milk, along with that of Guernseys, yielding the highest butter-fat content. Often their smooth flanks are the same color as the cream they produce. Men and women come to resemble the animals with which they work. Horsemen are quick of hands, body, and temper, for they work with quick, violent beasts, and are usually wiry, slender, tough. Those working with dairy (and even beef) cows are slower, quieter, heavier, because they deal with animals which are slower, quieter, blockier in build, except for the bulls with their great wrestlers' shoulders, their powerful legs, their deep-hanging brisket between the front legs. Charlie's bull was called "Grand View You'll Do." It was named for his farm, which was on top of an oak-covered hill southwest of Marion, Iowa, with a grand view in all directions of other fields and woods and even a distant look at Cedar Rapids.

Charlie was a typical dairy cattleman, soft-spoken, with no profanity (unlike the horsemen, who spat out cuss words like oats), strong but not aggressive; I've seen plenty of racehorse drivers fighting behind the barns, but no cattle exhibitors. In his blue overalls and blue cotton shirt Charlie would say to me on a late afternoon of my annual summer visit to the farm, "Come on, Paul. Let's go down to the barn and talk things over."

The only thing we had to talk over was talk, Charlie's favorite activity next to showing his dairy herd at county fairs. On the way to the barn, which was set into the north slope of the hill, so that I could climb onto its roof by stepping up from the ground, Charlie would say, "Now I want to take you down in the grove and show you how to handle a half nelson. Saw you wrestling that Schwarzwalder kid the other day. Never should have let him take you down. Better not do it here, the wife might not like it."

At the barn I would help drive the cows into their stalls while Charlie took pails and began to milk, sitting on his little three-legged stool and pulling the teats in a firm, gentle, stripping motion while the cats came purring around for their unearned share. Now and then he would squirt a stream directly into my mouth; it was warm, foaming, the taste itself nourishing. Charlie talked to me man to man. Jerking his head in the direction of a cow he would say, "Now take that Ethel over there"—he named all his cows and swore that they answered to their names; he spoke the word several times to each cow when milking, twice a day; even their thick skulls must have heard and remembered—"she likes to hold back her milk. Sometimes when I strip her at the end I get more than when I thought I was finished. June over there's a great breeder, calf every year."

One day he put the bull in the barnyard for some sun and exercise. Grand View You'll Do was a glowing brown-red mahogany color, his hide glistening and rippling as he walked. He had a heavy ring in the fleshy lip under his nose for leading. One day Charlie had emptied manure on the big pile in the barnyard and was headed for the door when he heard his bull charging behind him. He ran for the fence, closer than the door, but Grand View You'll Do caught him and threw him up in the air. If Charlie had landed in the yard he would have been trampled to death, but (I assume because of the saintliness of his character) he landed just on the other side of the fence. The bull pawed the ground, snorting, threatening, shaking his horns in frustration. Charlie got up, ribs bruised, pride hurt, ashamed to have been humiliated before an eight-year-old nephew. Most farmers would have sworn (any horseman kicked would have sworn), but Charlie just said to me, "Paul, anybody turns his back on a bull is a durn fool." I was shocked. The bull's action was a natural hazard of farming, but I had never heard Charlie say "durn" before.

I have since been in some well-built, beautiful, often over-whelming buildings: the Taj Mahal in Agra, the Meiji Shrine in Tokyo, Westminster Cathedral, the Parthenon in Athens, Notre Dame de Paris, the Vatican, the Great Mosque of La-hore (largest in the world). I have walked up inside the head of the Great Buddha of Kamakura, west of Yokohama. But Char-lie's cheap, thin, wooden, red barn on a farm in Iowa too small, its soil too sandy, was the greatest building in my life, because I was a boy haunting its haymow, sliding down the stored timo-thy and clover hay. If you haven't smelled a field of clover after it has been cut, the stems and the flowers bleeding the essence of their rich odor, your nose has been deprived. You have lived in a poverty of smell. Chanel, cry your heart out.

The curved roof of the haymow was my first look at a Gothic arch, long before I saw Chartres. Rituals took place in that barn — breeding, birthing, feeding, watering, milking, a little praying when a cow or sow had a bad delivery. I never smelled incense in any consecrated church so rich, so reward-ing, so physically addictive as the odors of cow and horse ma-nure, timothy and clover hay, oat straw, fresh milk, silage from the silo with its molasses–corn stalk mixture, animal body warmth, oiled harness leather, all blended together in one overwhelming, enriching gift to the nose. Charlie loved it. When he walked into the barn he would stop and inhale deeply. "Just as good as breakfast, Paul," he told me. "Sets me up for the day. If I could bottle it I'd sell it. Couldn't fill the demand." It was a holy place for me; what we worshipped there was the animal and plant life that nourished human life. I was lucky, as a city kid, to feel at home with that manure and that hay.

Charlie took me down to the hickory grove that morning after chores. It was a sacred grove for me because I had my wrestling lessons there out of sight of Aunt Gertrude, his wife, who didn't like him teaching me tricks, and it was the source of the nuts which she made into hickory-nut cakes. That is the most painful cake, because the hickory is the hardest nut to crack. Its shell is like iron, so we had to crack the nuts on the floor by laying them on a sadiron and pounding them with a hammer. The nut never came out whole like a soft-shell pecan, so that even when it was split we had to take the meat out with thin, sharp picks, an hours-long job. But hickory nuts are the sweetest of all, made even sweeter because we had earned that cake by the labor of climbing the tree and shaking its branches, gathering the nuts in pails, stripping off their thick green hulls, drying them, and wrestling to get the meat out, so many making just a cup of the inner kernels for the cake.

Charlie crouched under the trees, his broad shoulders swaying, his long arms swaying, his hands up and ready. "Now remember, Paul," he told me in his quiet voice, "a man coming at you fast is a little off balance. You can use his weight and speed to throw him. Get a foot behind his knee. Come at me, Paul."

I rushed him in a kid's impulsive way. In a second I was flat on my back with the wind knocked out of me.

Charlie helped me up. "Now the thing about the Strangler was, if you got a scissors lock on his neck with your legs, he could swell up his neck muscles and slide out of it. You had to get behind him and grab his arms and hang on and hang on. Like this."

He spun me around, knocked me down, pushed both arms up along my back by the wrists. "You can break a man's arm that way if you shove hard enough. Of course, you need a little more meat on your bones than you've got." He jerked me up by my spindly arms, waited a moment, and then said, "Sometimes you can catch a man in a cradle." He grabbed me, one arm between my legs, twisted me in a full circle in the air, and lowered me to my feet gently.

"You shoulda took my arm and turned me around and tripped me up," Charlie warned me. "That's enough today. Let's fill this bucket and take some nuts to the house. Maybe we can talk the wife into a cake."

Talking to me about wrestling, Charlie always used the word "man" to describe the skinny incompetent he was teaching. It gave me a sense of the power I would never have.

Down under the hickory trees I learned the manly art of

self-defense (Charlie always said a wrestler could always beat a boxer because he wouldn't let him use his fists), and I learned about the sweetest nuts in the world.

What more do you want out of a small grove on a small and not very productive farm in eastern Iowa? What kid had it all, as I did?

Charlie's Jersey herd was a fine one. He won ribbons at every fair he entered. He won so many that he had them sewn onto a blanket, the big blue rosettes for champion cow or bull at the top, and threw it over Grand View You'll Do to wear in the livestock parade down the racetrack at the Monticello Great Jones County Fair. One year the bull was declared Grand Champion. I watched while Charlie led the parade, holding a piece of pipe hooked into the ring on Grand View You'll Do's nose. The bull swung his head as he walked, not out of bad temper, but to show that he really was a powerful animal, a true champion. Watching from the stands with my family, my little strength seemed to swell within me. I had wrestled Charlie. Now he was wrestling that bull. He walked on into the shadows by the cattle barns, the robe of ribbons glowing in the dark.

In the Depression, Charlie lost his farm, part of which my grandfather had been given for being a cavalryman in the Civil War. I went to the auction of all the farm equipment. It was hideous. Charlie and I stood listening to the buzzsaw voice of the auctioneer knocking down the stuff Charlie had spent a lifetime of grinding work buying and using—the walking plow for the cornfield where he raised the feed for his horses, cattle, and hogs during the winter; the wagon in which we hauled the vegetables to sell at the Farmer's Market in Cedar Rapids: the pumpkins he harvested in the cornfield after the stalks were chopped, the melons in summer (steel runners replaced the wagon wheels for trips into town in winter); the feed grinder I used to turn by hand before we slopped the hogs; the harrow, the disc, the mower, the hay rake, all horse-drawn; the harness into which I had helped Charlie rub the neat's-foot oil that kept it supple, kept it from drying and cracking; the pitchfork for hay, the scoop for manure, the garden hoe, the spade polished with thousands of thrusts into the soil; the old pony saddle my cousins rode. No tractor, no truck—it was too early in the century and the farm too small.

Charlie watched as each of the items his tough hands had handled for years was held up, or walked around, as the auctioneer described it in his swift-flowing patter. Charlie hunched forward, balancing on the balls of his feet, alert, ready, but lost. He could grapple with any man but not with a first and a second mortgage and the invisible enemy of debt.

He would not walk again to that barn for chores, nor put a ten-gallon cream can in the cold water at the little dairy house to cool, nor make his deliveries from house to house in Cedar Rapids to very special customers who appreciated the extra richness and freshness of his milk. He would stop at our house halfway for a cup of coffee, a piece of Mother's pie. (Mother never bought a pie, a roll, or a loaf of bread in her life; they were all baked in our crazily designed kitchen.) My mother and Uncle Charlie, sister and brother, had that generous Reinheimer quality, loved to sit and talk, to share food and affection. Charlie would say, "Paul, when are you coming out to the farm? I could use a good man right now. June and Mary are about to calve any day now. They usually come in at night, there's some fence to fix, I got a new hold to show you." Losing his farm was like losing his life, but he never complained. Not even at the auction.

Charlie went into the farm kitchen at the end, put his arms on the table, laid his head on his arms, and wept.

UNCLE BILLIE

Billie was my father's racehorse brother. Like most horsemen, he was lean, hard, quick in every action, profane, a hard drinker (Charlie never touched a drop, nor did Herm), ready to fight any time anyone questioned his skill, his word, or his right to his own space. He was a wonder with horses and a bastard with people. He lived at the fairgrounds, usually in a little room off the horse barn which could be heated with a coal stove, and traveled from fair to fair during the season, racing trotters and pacers. His wife, Rachel, was short and strong, a fine horse handler who would get into the sulky seat and jog each of the horses every day. After the races, she would lead them around in circles, blanketed, to cool them down. She was expert at putting liniment or a heating ointment on a leg to reduce the swelling.

Billie and Rachel traveled in an ancient Reo truck hauling the horses, the sulky tied on the back. They parked it near the horse barn, stabled the horses, swept out the truck, washed it down, and lived in it while at the fair, with a mattress on the floor and a little kerosene stove on the ground. The harness hung from pegs on the inside of the truck. Long before the day of the "mobile home" they had one, shared with the animals that supported them. The support was bad. Billie had only a few months of racing in the Midwest to make enough money for the whole year. Even if he won some good purses, feed for the horses, food for the two of them, harness repairs, veterinarian bills (almost no bills for doctors: they took horse medicine when they got sick), and heating in the winter took it all, and usually more than all. Many late autumns they would arrive in the truck and drop off the horses at Father's barn for him to feed all winter.

I soon learned the difference between racing animals and saddle animals; the latter were more disciplined, quieter, more used to being handled under pressure; the former were wilder, more fiery, more nervous. One entire winter I rode Billie's pacer, a gray-white mare named Faybelle with a record time of 1:59.5, taking her out to a country road of hard sand and a mile-long straightaway. I had ridden three-gaited and five-gaited show horses on a moderate single-foot and a fast rack, but never at such speeds. I've flown jets around the world and driven a four hundred–horsepower car wide open on the raceway along Daytona Beach in Florida, but neither had the feeling of the surging speed of the pacer. The others were mechanical. Faybelle was alive; I could feel the motion of each leg and of that long-muscled back. At thirty miles an hour, one leg on each side of that great, throbbing chest, hearing the breath inhaled hard through the flared nostrils, the wind beating my face, my hands sensed through the leather reins the pressure of the steel bit in Faybelle's mouth. "Ride 'em with your hands, Paul," my father told me. "You can tell how they're doing. Steady, easy. Steady, easy. And talk. Let 'em know you're there. Don't yell. Soft hands, soft voice make a soft mouth."

The bit was a snaffle, swiveling in the middle, unlike the solid curb bit with a chain under the lip. The snaffle was the gentlest bit, best for the mouth, but if the horse was wild or bad-tempered (not by nature, but from bad handling), the snaffle wouldn't control it.

The pace is a learned gait. In a trot, left front and right rear hooves hit the ground together and leave it together, right front and left rear hooves the same. The pace is like the single-foot but far faster; the rider is carried on a long, floating motion. Faybelle took me down that road as if I were airborne.

Many racehorses are not saddle trained, but Faybelle was. When Uncle Billie brought her to our barn, he said, "Now Paul, she's saddle broke. Ride 'er. Keep 'er in shape, make 'er extend herself so she'll be able to jump into training in the spring and I can get the jump on those other nags that have been loafing around barns all winter."

Feed to Billie's racehorses meant food out of the mouths of the Engle family; so that they could have enough oats, we ate more bland oatmeal. We believed in this, it was a family matter, that was how one poor family helped a member who was poorer. It was very Chinese: they were a people who gave me examples of the power of the family to give trust, security, and love to each other.

There wasn't much security or love in Uncle Billie, whose motto was, "Hit 'em first. It confuses 'em." I never saw him mistreat an animal, just a few men, and they probably deserved it. There are as many rough characters as tough horses around those barns.

It was Billie who taught me about stimulants for man and

beast. After all the races were over and the horses cooled, watered, and fed, we would go to the ancient Reo and he would fix his favorite drink. It was Prohibition, so a lot of inventing was done. Rachel would buy a bottle of female tonic, which she didn't need, she was healthy; it had a high alcohol content. Then Billie would strengthen it with alcohol bought from a bootlegger, put in ice, and he had a powerful, herb-flavored cocktail. Soon the truck air would be fragrant with herbs and alcohol. Billie would relax after the intensity of the racing heats, the close shaves with other sulkies, the swearing at other drivers trying to cut in on him, and the tiring effort of holding on to a fast-moving animal while mentally calculating how much strength it had in it after three quarters of a mile of total racing and whether the whip or his voice could get one more burst of speed at the end of the straightaway after the oval track. Billie was very clever at pacing a horse, at getting the last-second increase in speed without the horse breaking stride. This is the heart of race driving; if pushed too hard, an animal will jump out of its pace or trot and run. Even if it crosses the finish line in first place, it is disqualified if it is not on its gait. Billie could force a pacer to its fastest stride while — by a skillful use of his hands on the reins, and so on the bit, and a controlling chant of his voice — keeping it from going off its gait.

Billie shared his taste for drink with his horses. I have seen him take an exhausted horse behind the barn, and while I helped hold its mouth open he would put a long syringe deep in its mouth and shoot aromatic spirits of ammonia down its throat to give it enough stimulus for the next race. The horses loved it, prancing, lively. Next heat!

Rachel was swarthy and spoke an accented English. The family always said she was part Indian. Bending over her tiny stove in the evening, the sun setting red because of the dust from the fairgrounds behind her, stirring a pot full of onions, potatoes, carrots, cabbage, a chunk of pot roast simmering, her dark hands stirring, she would talk to the stew. Fresh from cooling down the horses, she looked as if she had just come from one of the western tribes. She was good to me. With no children of her own, she liked having me around, giving me her folk wisdom (or were they Indian proverbs?)— "Stew's like people, Paul, don't rub too much salt on it." "If a horse steps on your foot, don't beat it. Just pick up its hoof." "Horses are like women. Talk to 'em. Don't just grab 'em." "If it don't have onions in it, it ain't food." "Billie never started a fight, but he never ran away from one." "When you've got a green horse and he's in a fast race, sing to 'im. It'll settle 'im down. Especially a mare."

Billie talked less. He sat with us while Rachel cooked, nursing his female-tonic cocktail, resting from the races, saying, "That was a tough one, Paul. Son of a bitch tried to jam in front of me on the curve. Know what I did? I took the whip and cut him a good one across the back of his neck. The judges couldn't see because we were on the far side behind the trees." He laughed, which he did rarely. "Bastard was so surprised he raised his arms and threw that chestnut gelding off its stride and had to pull to the outside so he was out of the heat." He took a long drag on his fancy drink and added, "Don't go around looking for a fight. But don't take no crap from anybody."

Like horses, Billie and Rachel were a good team. By the strict Methodist standards of our family, they were a wild outfit, never went to church, cussed, drank, and were rumored to be friendly to each other in bed. They lived on the edge of poverty but were rich in harness, sulkies, the language of horses. The lean Billie and the round Rachel went from fair to fair trying to survive in a life that was seldom fair. They would give you their last dollar and would happily take yours. Once Billie staggered drunk up the sidewalk to our house, and Mother used the word "damn" for the only time in her life. She felt Billie was bad company for her husband because of the booze, the violence, and his dislike of "nice" women. She also sensed that a little of Tom's small annual income ran away into Billie's pocket; she was right to feel that he was a menace to the security of her family.

I got along fine with Uncle Billie. He talked to me man to
man, giving me advice that was often some years ahead of my
experience: "Paul, look out for the woman who takes your
pants down. Chances are she isn't looking for what you think,
she's looking for your billfold." "Never water a horse after a
race until he's cooled down. Throw the water on him." "The
secret's in the shoeing. You can ruin a horse's leg if you put too
heavy a toe weight on. Blacksmith's just as important as the
driver." "Don't use tobacco. Liquor's okay. God never in-
tended you should drag hot smoke down your throat and into
your lungs, but he did intend you should pour liquids down
your throat and into your guts." Having invoked God's blessing on his female tonic, he took a long swallow, followed by a
sigh that came all the way up from his guts. "Paul, one thing
about horses—you can't tell what they're going to do by looking. If you go near a horse, put a hand on him. That way if he's
going to kick you can feel the muscles getting ready." "Ain't no
horses born mean, just a lot of bastards make 'em that way."
"Now about women"—I'd waited years for this advice—
"they're a great invention, but tougher to handle than horses
because you can't put a bit in their mouth or use a whip on
their rump. There's two kinds—them that complain because
they think you want it too much and them that complain they
don't get enough. Not much you can do about either kind except calm 'em down. Cool 'em off. Walk 'em around."

Like most horsemen, including my father, Billie had narrow
hips. He had the same gesture as Tom, putting both elbows on
his hips, pulling his trousers up when they slipped. To see the
two of them facing each other, talking, jerking their trousers
up with their elbows, talking louder than was necessary for
people so close, swearing and threatening as if their ordinary
conversation was sure to end in a fight, both stinking of horse
manure, their hands leaping in the air without stopping, made
me feel I was living with my own kind. It was years before I
found people who didn't cuss every other word, who didn't
smell, who talked softly—dull, no vigor, no smell, no wild-
ness. They both ran headlong at life and at other people. If

they ran over you, too damn bad, look where you're going. (What they really meant was, Look where *I'm* going!)

For their size, the three brothers, Billie, Herm, and Tom, were very strong. My father weighed about 130 pounds, but I have seen him throw hundred-pound bales of hay. Billie was the smallest, the feistiest, the most violent, the most profane, the most irreverent ("Church is for sissies"), the harshest in speech and action, and the most erotic. (Tom and Herm never talked about women to me, but Billie did — as if, at the age of eight, I could understand, which flattered me — and I wish now, at age seventy-two, I could ask him a few questions.) Tom and Herm lived safe, conventional, working lives, but wild man Billie outlived them by ten years. Never underestimate the rewards of sin.

When Billie was eighty he still drove trotters and pacers. He hated Social Security and welfare: "Ain't nobody going to pay me for not working. I'm going to hang in there until the last second. When I can't handle a horse in a tough race, let me die. I'm not scared, but I'll miss the ladies."

Hiawatha and My Aunt Bertha

I cannot look at the poem "Hiawatha" without being reminded of my aunt Bertha, for on her first visit to our home after marrying my uncle Jasper she brought me a copy of Longfellow as a gift. Since it was the only book of verse she was ever known to have, I could never understand how she happened to give it to me. One might have expected some pious poems on the relationship between God and a small boy and the devil — for I had just put some marbles in the new bride's bed, with the most interesting results. I never did grasp why the gesture should have been punished so severely, for they were my best snot-agates.

Now, however, looking back through the wilderness of time with an eye sharpened on the Deerslayer and the Lone Ranger, I can see at last why Aunt Bertha gave me a poem written in a Finnish meter by a New England poet about an Ojibway Indian wooing a girl in the primeval forest of America. She saw her own romantic wooing symbolized in it.

Like Hiawatha, my uncle Jasper had bravely gone into the great West for his bride, out to the Black Hills of South Dakota. Like the Indian's family in the poem, my uncle's family urged him to marry a nice neighbor girl and not a savage maiden from an enemy tribe. Uncle Jasper first saw Bertha when he went to make a horse deal with her father, who did not chip arrowheads of chalcedony like the father of Minnehaha, but who did make business deals sharp enough to split the ribs and pocketbook of an innocent young warrior like my uncle. Bertha had smiled shyly at Jasper while extending to him her ring finger. (According to my father, that finger had been tenderly held out toward unmarried men for nineteen years before my uncle arrived, but Father had little romance and much bad digestion.) Jasper returned home with a broken-winded nag, leaving a broken heart out in the Black Hills.

Now there was no peace for Jasper in that land, neither in hunting the fallow deer nor fishing for the speckled trout, nor even in his favorite sport (favorite because it could be done sitting down) of checking the bloodlines of trotters. So Jasper put on his moccasins, turned his face to the dangerous West, and bought a ticket on the Northwestern to Buffalo Gap.

Uncle did not arrive at the wigwam of his beloved with the carcass of a red roebuck slung over his shoulder like Hiawatha. Instead, he brought a handsome gold locket on the cover of which was engraved a fat mare grazing on gold grass and fatly watching a young colt which seemed to be walking on its front legs. (My mother considered this a mite forward as a gift for a young lady; my father agreed that it would be, if the lady were young; my mother's glare then throttled him for the rest of the evening.) At the moment of Jasper's arrival, Bertha's father, the ancient Arrow-maker, was whipping a two-year-old thorough-bred into shape in the corral, and Bertha was whipping a four-layer cake into shape in the kitchen. Jasper was received with open arms by Bertha and with open mouth by her father who, however, regained his composure when Bertha "gave them drink in bowls of bass-wood," as was the custom in the land of the Dacotahs.

All evening Uncle Jasper sat and listened, on the front porch of the house that looked west toward Wind Cave National Park, to the old Arrow-maker declaiming of the days when the country had been filled with noble warriors, when men were men, and the few women were glad they were. But today, he deplored, looking fiercely over his moustaches at Jasper, that "the men were all like women, only used their tongues for weapons."

However feeble a specimen Uncle Jasper may have been, and however frail his weapons, he broke through the old gen-tleman's resistance with devastating and suspicious ease. When he turned to Bertha, as that discreet maiden sat back in the shadows which made her seem only twice her size, he softly asked if she would go east with him from the land of her ances-tors as his bride, over meadow, mountain, hill, and hollow. Her answering "Yes" came with sudden sureness, as if it issued not simply from her throat but from the remote Wind Cave itself, gathering power as it swept through stormy gorge and along grassy slope. So the old proud frontiersman shook Uncle's hand in a grip that seemed to remove it from the wrist in one piece, and without a tear in his eye commented that this was the fate of fathers and he would bear it as hardily as he had endured the blizzards and the suns of the old days of Indian Territory and Calamity Jane. Always, he said, "comes a youth flaunting feathers" and lures the village daughters far away.

On the homeward trip it could not be said of Uncle Jasper that "in his arms he bore the maiden; Light he thought her as a feather." For what Uncle had thought, sitting on the porch in the dark of the evening, to be half shadow and only half Bertha turned out to be all Bertha. But he was always a man for keeping a filly in good flesh, and this additional presence seemed only to double his good fortune.

Uncle brought his bride not to a lodge of hemlock branches but to a little place on the edge of town. There were trees around it, however, and his new wife could still feel at home, for out of them "peeped the squirrel, Adjidaumo, Watched with eager eyes the lovers; And the rabbit, the Wabasso."

It was soon after moving there that Aunt Bertha came to visit us and brought me the book that still stands on the shelf above my desk. When *you* see that book, it is probably the shy and copper-dusky face of Minnehaha which peers out of the pages. For me, it is the gay and pancake-patted face of Aunt Bertha, telling us, with the vigorous gestures of the frontier, how Uncle Jasper faced with the courage of youth the barbed and barbarous arrows of her father's tongue, and all for her.

It was wonderful what she did for Uncle Jasper, who had been, up to the time of his marriage, a rather gloomy soul like my father, suspicious of people who laughed very much, on the perfectly sensible grounds that the world was too grim a place for laughter in itself, and so there must be some sinister motive behind anyone who laughed. To my father, it meant that the other guy in a deal was getting the best of him and laughing about it in advance and to his face, and that was too humiliating to bear. Besides, he had once bought a sorrel gelding from a jovial individual who slapped him on the back and roared and chuckled through a whole morning until he had my father's money and the animal, a genuinely fine-looking creature, was in the barn. My father gloated and strutted in his subdued way until he went into the stall to feed and water the horse, which suddenly lost its gentleness, kicked out a sideboard, knocked my father down, and, rankest betrayal of all, turned and sneered at him in a horse-laugh that was a raucous parody of its former owner's.

Under Bertha's beneficent influence, Uncle Jasper himself would now and then make strangled laughing noises in his throat, as if a trap had just snapped on a mouse inside him and the death-struggle was on. My father always ridiculed the meaning of Minnehaha, Laughing Water, by referring to Bertha as "giggle-girdle," but he only used this phrase once in her presence, for she turned to him and said in a tone of sweet devastation, "How did you know?" At this point Uncle Jasper collapsed in his chair, wrestling weakly with the snorts and trumpetings in his throat, so I had to rush out of the house and get a bucket of cold well-water to revive him.

Even at the distance of my room's width, and on a shelf of bright bindings, I can still pick out that volume of Longfellow in its dull green cloth with dim gold letters. And seeing it there, I am once again back in Bertha's kitchen (her favorite room in the house and, when she was in it, mine too), watching her solid hands bend to a mixing bowl and listening to her voice, which was as smooth, no matter what she was talking about, as the plump, pink skin on her neck. She would pour the words out the way she poured batter from a bowl, in a rich, raisin-running stream. Now and then she would be overcome by emotion at the thought of having a home and a husband and a hungry nephew who had an untamed finger for scraping the inside of a pan. At such times she would turn to me, the hair draggled over her slightly sweating face, one hand still stirring the batter and the other held toward me as if offering a cookie and her heart in one supreme gesture. Then she would quote from *the* poem: "Love is sunshine, hate is shadow, Life is checkered shade and sunshine, Rule by love, O Hiawatha!"

I was a wonderful audience, for I never interrupted, partly out of real affection for this woman who was the first one to treat me as if I actually was a male, and partly because that would have slowed down the processes that led to my getting at the scraping of the dish in which the icing was being made. I did honor her by reading the book, however, and I could even quote a snatch back at her when the moment demanded. Looking beyond her through the kitchen window to the barnyard, I could see Uncle Jasper hustling through the checkered shade and sunshine, unaware of the affectionate language about him that was hovering in the kitchen like the sweet odor of baking.

The trouble with the few lines I recalled from Hiawatha was that they never seemed to fit any situation. When Aunt Bertha was describing the glories of being wooed by Uncle Jasper, flinging out her arms in a dramatic gesture so broad that no one could fail to be guided directly to her expansive and loving bosom, proving to me Jasper's accurate aim in catching this proud bird on the wing, how could I sit calmly on my tall stool by the wood-range and say: "Shot the wild goose, flying southward, On the wing, the clamorous Wawa"?

There was one gay evening when Aunt Bertha read aloud a long section from the poem. This was in absolute defiance of my father, who distrusted all books with the argument that it was a sneaking thing for a man to write a book, because no one could be on the spot, before the book got written, to show him how wrong he was. That was a painful handicap for an arguing man like my father. But this night Bertha, elevated by a pat that Uncle Jasper had given her with his massive paw, asked me to run to my room and get the book. With Father glaring from his stationary rocker, which he agitated back and forth in a domestic war dance, Bertha read the pages about Hiawatha's wooing. Jasper sat in a clouded state of mind, proud of his literary woman, but wishing she had chosen to read something more obviously safe than poetry.

Bertha droned on in a schoolgirl's sing-song until she came to the part about the ancient Arrow-maker in the land of the

Dacotahs, sitting at the doorway of his wigwam, "making arrow-heads of jasper." My father jerked to a stop, paused a second to fix a glittering eye on Uncle Jasper (who looked like a scared woodchuck about to dive down his hole, only there wasn't any hole), then threw up his left arm in the shape of a bow, with his right arm fitted an imaginary arrow, drew a careful bead on Jasper's disintegrating dignity, and with a war whoop drove the arrow of his scorn into his brother's vitals. It was not a fatal wound, but it left a lifelong scar; on rainy evenings of reading it would ache and throb and I could see Jasper bearing his pain bravely, while calculating the exact area of my father's scalp-lock that could be cut off in one savage stroke of the knife.

None of this bothered Bertha, who read with a stronger voice, entranced that she now had my father's complete interest. She gradually came to the lines that the moon speaks to Hiawatha and Minnehaha as the delirious couple is on its journey homeward from the west to Hiawatha's own people:

> Day is restless, night is quiet,
> Man imperious, woman feeble;
> Half is mine, although I follow;
> Rule by patience, Laughing Water!

At the line "Man imperious, woman feeble," Jasper miraculously recovered from the treacherous blow my father had given him, leaped to his feet, and shouted imperiously to Bertha, "Woman, stop that noise." And still in the fullness of his male pride, triumphing over his wife and my father in a single action, he ordered, "Get your hat, we're going." Before any one could protest, he seized Bertha's vast hat, which had more feathers on it than a warbonnet, clapped it on his wife's head, and steered her out of the house, dropping a grin of victory in my father's lap, thrusting it there like a tomahawk.

So they swept from the room, Bertha's feathers flying as if once again back on a living wing. We never finished that poem. But on any occasion when my mother would ask my father to do something for her that was a little outside the male line, like helping her in the house, Uncle Jasper would draw a sudden blanket around him, throw back his head, and, pointing his fat finger, would declaim, "Man imperious, make it snappy."

Like the skulking coyote of the plains, Father would slink from the room and lurk out of sight until his self-respect and courage had been restored. I had to keep the book in my room, hidden, or Father would have burned it. That, too, may have given me a deeper attachment to it, for we shared a common danger, although my burning would have been more local and less deadly than the book's.

Uncle Jasper and Aunt Bertha and my father have gone to the happy hunting grounds. Aunt Bertha and Minnehaha are in the shade under a pin oak tree comparing women's notes while keeping a sharp eye on Uncle Jasper and Hiawatha, who are fishing in waters forever untroubled and forever well-stocked with trout. My father is rocking gaily on a porch, now and then hitting a burst of speed as he thinks of some shocking episode in the mortal past.

I sit here reading the poem and finding in it a story of which bearded Longfellow never dreamed, proud of my own land's history that could have in it such glories as Hiawatha's accurate arrows and Minnehaha's voice liquid with Dacotah laughter. Proud, too, of Aunt Bertha's pride in her cookies (black walnut, sweet with autumn frost, yum) and her husband, of Uncle Jasper's gallant wooing, and of my father's contempt for dead books and his conceit for his blooded horses.

My parents

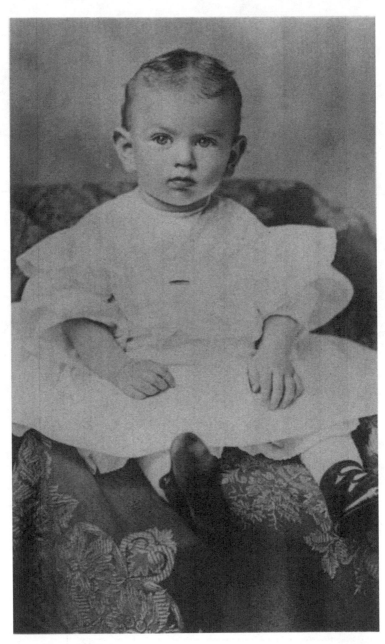

Myself as an infant

My sister Alice and I

My sister Kathryn and I
Opposite above: The house in Cedar Rapids
where I was born and grew up
Opposite below: My mother

Grandfather Jacob Reinheimer
in full uniform . . .

. . . and I in mine

Uncle Charlie
Uncle Billie

Fishing (I'm on the left) in the Cedar River

In front of my father's "Riding Academy"

My father and I

A high school portrait

The Glory of the Senses

The senses of our tough but delicate bodies seemed to be tougher and more delicate earlier in this century than today. I remember it as a more sensuous time, when we lived closer to the physical world enriching our nose, hands, ears, eyes, and tongue. Many of the smells, touches, sounds, sights, and tastes have wholly disappeared or are rare, the lost enrichment of our lives. Of course, horses still exist in the country, but they are not carrying people on city streets or plowing fields. How many horses do you see each day? When I was a kid, every day we saw those handsome animals trotting, heard them whinnying, knew their many smells.

SMELLS

Our neighborhood butcher shop, run by Jack and his family, Czechs not long from the old country, made their own sausages, hams, and bacon. The smell of hickory mingled with melted fat drifted over the street, and all the kids came running. The butcher's face was red and round and cheerful, proving the value of the meat he sold. "Go on, kids, stick your head in," he would shout. We opened the smokehouse door, stuck our heads between the fire on the floor and the meat hanging from the ceiling, and breathed deeply, smelling the wood smoke and the heated pork, one of the earthy delights. Then we pulled our heads out, choking with smoke, eyes full of stinging tears, and slammed the door. Each kid (including two girls of great courage) dared the ritual, which gave them membership in the 4th Avenue and 16th Street Club of Smokesmellers. The odor of that curing meat was so strong we could taste it on the tongue. Now we have frozen TV pork, and richness falls away from our mouths.

There was the great autumn burning of the leaves in piles along the street, filling the air with an exciting tang. Cities now ban that brilliant smell, so absurdly replaced with fumes of the auto engine. We would dare each other to run through the smoke until our clothes were permeated with the essence (as with a perfume) of burning leaves. We had to hang them outdoors for days until they were deodorized and fit for school. I resented having that luxurious smell, which money could not buy, treated as if it were the vile odor of skunk. Autumn has kept its glowing light but lost its glamorous pleasuring of the nose. It is marvelous that the original meaning of "smell" was to burn slowly, to give off smoke. Now the leaves make their graceful fall in the American fall and end up in garbage bags.

Mother always made sauerkraut in October, along with dill and sweet pickles. The air in the kitchen vibrated with odors, each enhancing the other: cabbage cooking with its spices, small cucumbers seething in their brine, the always-present soup kettle simmering on the back of the range (ours was accurately called a "Smoke Eater"), the range itself giving off that odor of hot iron which has disappeared from our lives. How busy our noses were in those years. I remember lifting the lids of the pots with the dill pickles and the sauerkraut and sniffing that spicy scent of the herbs, the cucumbers and cabbage both raised in our own garden, the dill weed picked by our small hands from the lane leading from the dirt road in the country up to the oak-crowned hill of the farm where Mother and Uncle Charlie had been born.

Mother had sadirons, solid metal plates heated on the range and picked up by a special handle. Mother always heated them to iron her blouses or "shirt waists" when she was going to church or a marriage or a gathering of neighborhood ladies. The smell of starch as she pressed that cloth is still in my nose. It hovered around my mother whenever she was going to a special affair. "Hot Iron and Starch"—what a great name for a fragrance. Mother, I would like to smell you now as I did when I was six, resting my head on that sadiron-starched blouse under which was the breast that had nourished a baby named Paul. For years I thought that it was the breast which smelled of ironed starch.

One autumn Mother took a big crock of sauerkraut down to the cellar and left it there to "work," with a heavy rock on the lid to keep the fermentation going. Weeks later we were eating dinner (cabbage, of course, with chopped ham) when there was a tremendous thud in the living room. "Good God," Father shouted, "the piano fell through the floor!"—the disaster he had been predicting ever since Mother had managed to buy an old upright with scraps of money saved from the groceries. I ran into the living room and banged the piano keys to show it was still there. "Maybe the furnace exploded," Father said. "Paul, go down in the cellar and see. If you need me, yell."

The sauerkraut had exploded, banging the rock against the living-room floor. When I went down the cellar steps I could smell the salty tang of the kraut and see it on the ceiling, on the floor, over the jars of peaches and tomatoes Mother had canned at summer's end. I rushed upstairs with the dramatic news. Tom never wasted words. His only comment was, "Get some rags. Go down and clean it up." For days my hands smelled with the sour odor of kraut fermented too long.

There was also a cave down below called the root cellar where we stored cabbages, carrots, turnips, and potatoes, covering them with fine dirt. When uncovered, they had a fine fresh smell that I would breathe in deeply, thinking of the garden where I had planted, hoed, and weeded them in the summer. They were old friends, keeping a live odor in the house.

The first thing to penetrate the house in early morning was the odor of Czech sausage from our butcher shop, full of herbs and smoke. Father left at 6 A.M. each day for the horse barn, so he always had the same breakfast of meat and pancakes.

There was a little alcove at the end of our kitchen where he put his coat, jacket, gloves, and hat when he came home from the horse barn. His clothes were saturated with the strong smell of horse manure, which he had spent the day shoveling, and gradually it joined the other kitchen scents, the chili sauce with its hot pepper, the pickles with dill weed smelling of the sunlight in the hot lane where I padded barefoot through the sand to gather it, the big winter pot of soup always at the back of the range, into which extra vegetables and beef were thrown constantly, the cinnamon in the applesauce when Mother was in her violent home-canning phase. When the Smoke Eater was really fired up with coal and wood, she used the whole top for the jars of food that would feed the family all winter. I am sure some of the manure smell that had been hanging in the air since our house was built permeated the food and gave it that subtle tang which no food has had since. Even our cellar smelled of horse manure, blended with sauerkraut and coal smoke from the furnace, when Mother washed Tom's clothes. What lucky noses we had. Now I breathe a neutral air and eat homogenized food.

Mother had one drawer of her dresser where she kept her few really "nice" things — neck yokes, camisoles (do they exist any longer?), blouses, handkerchiefs edged with embroidery, a corset with lace worn only on great occasions such as marriages and christenings. Scenting the drawer was a sachet containing violet-fragrant powder. Mother would open the drawer and let me sniff the delicate odor of spring flowers coming from a cheap dresser in an ugly bedroom of a draughty wooden house in a bitter Iowa winter on an avenue called 5th and a street called 16th.

Of course, when Mother had the range up to a high heat, the smell of wood and coal burned the kitchen air. Then she would always bake bread, and when she opened the oven door, the shiny brown fragrance overwhelmed all the other kitchen odors and even crept upstairs to the bedroom, bringing a warm smell to those unheated rooms. Waking in winter to that nourishing odor was like waking in the black and the chill to the touch of a loved person, gaining hope and strength for the coming day. Half asleep, I crept downstairs in the half-dark, breathing in my breakfast. "Paul," Mother said, "you can eat the first heel on the loaf."

Even if the acrid smell of kerosene still stinks behind jet planes on airport runways, it has gone from the home. As evening softened daylight at the windows, Mother got out the kerosene lamps, asking me, "Paul, do you want to trim?" I took off the chimneys of glass, cleaned them with a soft rag, and then with sharp scissors cut off the black top of the wick, turning it up a little so that the clean part rose out of the kerosene in the base. Then came that cheerful moment when I scratched the match and held it to the wick, letting it burn until the flame flared across the whole top. I turned it down with a little wheel on the side and replaced the shining chimney; the yellow light, unlike an electric light bulb, filled the room with color and smell as well as illumination.

Aunt Minnie had a four-foot-high tapered glass vase on the floor of her living room. Each summer she filled it with rose petals, putting a frosted glass stopper in the top so that it was sealed. On days when I was an unnaturally good child, Minnie would say in a voice which hinted there must have been a ripsaw in her ancestry, "Paul, you're doin' fine today. You can smell the roses." I twisted out the stopper and put my nose to the vase, inhaling the fragrance while my eyes were caressed by the white, pink, red colors of the petals.

The exhaust fumes of a car travel out a tail pipe in the rear of a car and are left behind, the driver not knowing they are there. With a horse pulling a buggy or a sleigh, the opposite is true: its exhaust system is directly in front of the driver and passengers. The fumes go right into their faces. The wind and the droppings are only three feet away. Often when they came, Mother would be talking about flowers in her garden, or a dress, the children, cousins, church. She went on as if no explosion had taken place under her eyes and nose, as if that unique, rank odor had not suddenly polluted the neutral air. It was her life: a gentle voice in the midst of noise and stink.

At the barn Father had a huge manure pit that was my special responsibility. I not only filled it from the stalls but turned it while it was curing. Tom explained that horse manure is stronger than cow ("has more ammonia"), so that it had to be well rotted before it could be put on gardens; if fresh, it would burn the plants. Father had lively talks with several ladies about that rich stuff, which was always called "it." They would telephone to ask about its condition, and he would say, "Well, it's still a little hot. I'd give it a few weeks before you put it close to that zinnia bed."

After a few weeks my job came. We had a small, sturdy, quiet-tempered horse named Alice (my sister's name; I never knew if the horse was named for my sister or my sister for the horse). Alice was a fine animal—the horse, of course—and trotted stylishly under saddle. With her all-purpose qualities and size she must have had Morgan blood, Morgan that valuable New England horse named for Justin Morgan. I hitched up Alice to a wagon, filled it with "it," and drove across Cedar Rapids to the area where the richer families lived. Alice was skittish about clanging streetcars and honking autos, so I had to keep comforting her with my voice, as Tom had taught me. A bit in the mouth and leather reins will give a certain control, but Father's horses trusted the speaking human voice. I drove to the flower garden where the lady would be waiting. Putting on brown cotton gloves, she would tell me, "Paul, I want to check it," picking up a single turd, rubbing it between her fingers, and then sniffing it delicately. "Seems just right," she would tell me. "Do you have time to spread it?"

I took off Alice's bridle, put on a halter, and tied her to a tree; Tom did not allow a horse to be tied up with a steel bit in its mouth. Then I forked "it" (Father only used that term with ladies; in the barn it was horse shit) along the rows of flowers, with extra heavy amounts for the roses, but not letting any actually touch the plants. When I was done, the lady would look at her nourished garden, sniff the suddenly odorous air, and say, "Paul, it smells just right," and give me a dollar. "Do you want to take some flowers to your mother?" She cut the stems of zinnias, roses, asters, and dahlias and gave me an armful for home, where Mother separated them into vases or fruit jars, smelling the roses, which were wonderful, and the marigolds, which were awful.

There was the ghastly winter of the telephone poles. Because Father rented horses and specially equipped wagons to the telephone company, one autumn our backyard was filled with old and heavily creosoted telephone poles which had been replaced with new ones. It had been a bad year for Tom's horse business. He could hardly buy coal for the furnace, so he put a sawhorse (a "sawbuck") by the poles, gave me a bucksaw, and said, "Cut some up every day." A bucksaw has an H-shaped wooden frame with a blade at the bottom and a wire at the top to keep it taut. Its advantage is that you can operate it with both hands, making it especially useful for thick wood. Each day I dragged a pole between the upper arms of the sawbuck and worked that cutting blade back and forth until a piece twelve to eighteen inches long dropped off. The friction of the saw turned the wood warm, and the pungent smell of creosote poured from the pole. I carried the pieces down to the coal bin in the cellar. Father used them in the early morning because they caught fire faster than coal, which he added later. Again the tarry odor of creosote filled the air in the house and out-side. Today I shudder at the sight of a bucksaw and the scent of creosote. All winter I worked on those poles. They kept me warm while I sawed and when they burned in the furnace. What is an ordinary length of a tree trunk set in the ground and holding telephone wires was for me (and still is) the tough, dark enemy. I had begun to write poetry that year, and while pushing the saw back and forth I shaped lines of poems in the rhythm of the moving blade. The one virtue of smelling cre-osote today is that it reminds me of the way I cut language into lines, muttering to myself, as I cut that endless wood.

Neat's-foot oil — (made by boiling hooves and shinbones of cattle) — was another powerful scent in my childhood. Every autumn Tom brought the saddles, bridles, and harnesses from the barn to our basement, where we rubbed the yellowish oil into the leather to soften and preserve it. (Father didn't know where the name came from, but years later at Oxford Uni-versity I found out that "neat" was an Old English word for cattle.) The smell permeated the whole house as it escaped into the furnace and spread up the heat pipes. Even dinner those nights tasted like it. I even rubbed it into my boots and could sniff it sitting in school the next day.

Dry pine needles burned on our Christmas tree from a recklessly placed wax candle below it, with all the excitement to a child of possible catastrophe and the chance to yell "Fire!

Fire!" The resinous odor of burning pine right in the family parlor was a great and frightening joy.

There would be a field of red clover cut for hay and lying in the evening dew, the bruised stems sweet-smelling—sweeter than the timothy and alfalfa which have largely replaced it—as if the smell itself could nourish, without the stem and flowers.

I sold the *Cedar Rapids Gazette* on the corner of 3rd Avenue and 1st Street SE. Next to my corner (I assumed it was mine—no other newsboy dared intrude on it, at least not if he was smaller), where I howled the headlines of papers still redolent with wood pulp and fresh ink, was the tobacco store, in those days only a place for tobacco of every kind. It was dark, like the smell of Horseshoe Plug in heavy lead foil, filling the nose when it was cut with a sharp knife. A customer would buy a cigar, clip the end, put it in his mouth, then push a button at the tiny pilot light, and the fire would rise up for him to light his cigar, the fragrance of it filling the store. There were not many cigarettes in those days; it was mostly chewing tobacco and cigars. In the late afternoon I would make a last trip to the store before picking up the final edition of the *Gazette* for delivery to houses on my paper route in the east end of town. (I had toilet privileges from the old gentleman. I use the term *gentleman* advisedly: he always wore black sateen half sleeves, wrist to elbow, over his shirt.) The store would be dense with smoke and fragrant with burning tobacco. It was a store of and for men; I never saw a woman enter it. That smell was the sign of adult maleness. I inhaled it with pride and a marvelous sense of sin.

My nose has lost the glory of its smelling.

TOUCHES

I do not mean that all of these sensuous details have totally disappeared, only that they are no longer part of our daily life.

Leather reins were made from a once-alive skin which could twitch and had blood in it. If properly treated, they would keep the suppleness they had when the animal was eating, breathing, moving. The secret of handling a horse, whether it was pulling a buggy or wagon or was under saddle, was the sensitive impulse running from the bit in the mouth along the reins to the hands, and the quick adjustment made in pressure on the bit by the hands. There was a constant play back and forth between horse mouth and human hands, and the leather reins were a two-way communication line. There is no such sensitivity with a plastic steering wheel and car wheels, no living touch.

When Tom went to look at a saddle horse with an idea of buying, he first looked in the eyes, then at the teeth to check the age, then he felt the back of the lips where the bit's pressure came. I remember standing back and admiring the fine conformation of a chestnut gelding that stood with legs square and ears up. I said, "Dad, that's a beautiful one." "Not for us," he answered. In the car, out of earshot of the owner, he told me, "Hard mouth. Kids couldn't handle him."

It was through the reins that I could change a horse from a trot to a canter to a single-foot, with an inclination of the body and a tightening or loosening of the bit.

All praise to the corncob, that rough, inflammable thing. We kept wagonloads of them outside the house because they were wonderful for starting fires in the furnace after a cold night. There is no touch like it, with an occasional kernel of flinty field corn still left. They saved the sanitation for millions on farms and in small-town outhouses. ("Privy" seems too Latin for the actual use of those half-mooned little buildings so crucial to the farms of my childhood, including Uncle Charlie's.) The cobs felt a lot bumpier on some parts of the body than they did to the hand, but there were no daily newspapers delivered to farms, and we used what nature gave us. There was even a doll with a corncob as a body and a hickory nut for a face, with a lacy petticoat cut from an old corset cover — girls don't have it so fancy today.

In winter the family traveled by bobsled, a rough wagon body with wide steel runners replacing the usual wheels. Father would fill the bed with fresh oat straw, and the kids would burrow under it, feeling the long, smooth stems. Then he would throw an old buffalo robe over us, so we had another smoothness stroking us from above. When we touched the dense hair of that robe we touched the wild west; closing our eyes, we could feel the ground shake under the snow as an immense herd roared toward the wagon. Sometimes we would jump onto the runners; our feet trembled with their constant bumping over the rough ice and snow. The smell of fresh oat straw in winter!

Our long underwear was so coarse it made us itch, but the house was so badly heated we had to wear it indoors as well as out.

Charlie kept a big catfish in the stock tank by the barn. He had pulled it out of a deep hole where a tree had fallen across Indian Creek two miles away. I would reach down with my hand in the cool water and touch the soft gray skin. The fish would swim in wild circles. Once — I had been warned — it stabbed my hand with one of its sharp spines. When the cattle came to drink it would drop to the bottom and remain still. Exactly the color of the water, it was invisible. When the cattle left, it would swim to the surface and eat the bits of oats and corn they had left floating. Sometimes I would put my face down and stare at it closely, and it would stare back curiously for a moment before diving. The catfish is a very ancient creature, from a time before fish had scales. Watching it sink into a depth which might have been a hundred feet instead of four, I had a sense of primal life there in a dirty barnyard in Iowa.

There were far more thick calluses on people's hands because there was far more daily manual work. When Mother came at night in the dark to tuck me into bed, she always floated her hand over my forehead, and I felt that skin, toughened from a lifetime of handling hard things, from the time she was a girl on the farm. When I came back from Oxford, a soft-skinned place, and shook hands with my father, I was startled to find how rough the skin was on his hand, still handling pitchfork, manure scoop, hammer, axe, ears of field corn, reins of harness and bridle, every day of every week. The calluses came with the jobs of your life, the way pitted skin came with smallpox, and it never went away. I had the same calluses on my hands when I went to England and was at first surprised when I saw the shock in the eyes of those bright and decent upper-class (and occasionally titled) boys when they shook my working hand with their unworking hand.

I remember the sleekness of a horse's rump, soft as a woman's skin. The roughness of the mane and tail when I dragged a steel comb through them, removing the brittle cockleburs from the mane and the matted manure from the long tails. In summer when I worked around the horses they were steadily switching their tails to knock flies off their skins; often they would hit my face and make it tingle with their almost metal-like strength. They did not cut, but they stung.

Sometimes on very cold winter nights Mother would bring a brick wrapped in soft flannel and heated in the range to put at the foot of the bed for my toes. It was a marvelous, comforting touch, better than a pill to put one to sleep. But then there was the ordeal of the morning jump onto the freezing floor and the shivering of my feet as they walked across it. The suffering had one good effect: it woke me up instantly. I felt that cold to the top of my head. I was off and running, unlike some presidents, who have too much heat.

We traveled in those days, even for trips of a few miles, by slow trains with steam locomotives. Going to our Fuhrmeister relatives in Ely, perhaps six miles away, we took the Rock Island. The straight seats had a green plush fabric which tickled the back of my neck. It smelled of coal smoke.

Before this age of metal car, refrigerator, plane, we lived in a world of wood. To touch it was to sense the living tree from which it came rather than the lifeless iron or aluminum dug out of the ground and melted. We rode in a wooden wagon, buggy, or sleigh. We touched wood whenever we went downtown or to the horse barn or to the farm. The wagon was heavy boards for hauling heavy things. The buggy was light, with the wooden spokes whirling. The sleigh had that graceful curve of the dashboard curling back, and the steel runners were fastened to strips of wood. It was oak and hickory, tough. The baby buggy was wood, sometimes thin woven strips, very high, bouncing on springs. The touch of wood was the touch of our daily life. Uncle Charlie would gather branches from the hickory grove on his farm to smoke in their rich smell the pig he had raised and slaughtered himself. The hulls of black walnuts, butternuts, hickory nuts, and hazelnuts were all different, smooth to the touch but some hard, some soft. Under the hulls, after we had spread them to dry on the roof until they could easily be shucked off (with brown-stained fingers), was the toughness of the nuts. The black walnuts, sweetest of all, richest of all, had very hard shells. The surface was sharp, corrugated, rude. To get at the kernel inside we had to handle it, hold it, fight it, beat it. The hazelnuts grew on the hills outside Cedar Rapids. The nuts had a rough hull, but we used the stems for street hockey games with a tin can, because the roots made an abrupt right turn under the ground and made fine hockey clubs.

On the wall of my little bedroom I hung a hummingbird's nest still on the branch of a small tree. I cut it down in November, after it had been abandoned. I only saw it after the leaves had fallen, but then I knew where that emerald-throated hummingbird pair had spent the summer. Like them, it also was a jewel, but softer, moss-delicate inside. On winter mornings with a blizzard outside, the temperature twenty below zero, I would stroke it on waking up and feel the summer sunlight in it and the green throat of the tiny bird.

My hands have lost the glory of their touching.

SOUNDS

My childhood was a time of cheerful bells. In winter many people still traveled by sleigh, and ours not only had a long string of bells over the horse, it also had bells fixed to the shafts. One of the excitements was hearing in the distance the faint tinkling of a sleigh, giving us time to rush to the window and watch the horse trotting past with all its bells ringing ·

loudly, then fading as it disappeared. Why is the word "trot" important here? Because when trotting the left front and right rear hooves strike the ground, or snow, together, then the left rear and right front, so that the body of the horse continually lurches up and down, which is why a trot is rough to ride in a saddle unless you "post" with the moving rhythm of that powerful back beneath you, lifting your body up from the saddle with each of the steady lurches of the gait. At Christmas Mother hung a string of sleigh bells on the door so that our coming and going was celebrated by a sweet and metal clangor. Neighbors did not beat on the door, they shook the bells.

In summer the coming of the ice wagon was announced by a big brass bell, giving us kids time to run from alleys where we were playing hockey with hazel brush sticks and tin cans, or playing a game of marbles in the backyard, or weeding the family garden, and wait for the iceman to chip a fifty-pound chunk from a large block of ice and carry it with heavy tongs into the house. We scrambled for the little pieces of ice we could lick with our tongues or, on very hot days, rub on our foreheads.

Many steam trains ran through the center of Cedar Rapids, bells clanging as they neared downtown. Often several trains would be arriving or departing at the same time, so that the beating of bells would be coming close and going away together. They had great steam whistles, so much deeper and more musical than the horns on diesel trains. We could hear them in the early evening, and Father would say, "That's Northwestern 57 coming in from Omaha." When the engine slowed down and stopped, it would let off steam with a threatening snakelike hiss. When the train moved away, there was that hard sound of the drive shaft working to get such an immense weight of railroad cars moving, the steam escaping whitely from the cylinder, the engine grunting as it gained a little speed, the rumble and clatter as the cars shook with motion, the screech of iron wheels on iron rails.

We had a junk man who drove a rackety wagon and a rickety horse down the alley behind our house. He would cry out "I

buy all junk" in a rich Polish Jewish accent. He had a long
beard, eyes that shone like diamonds lost in a junkyard, and a
sharp feeling for children as well as for business. He wore a
round black hat that seemed to me both sinister and dignified.
His voice was what millions of immigrants had used in this
country, trying hard to communicate with these strange Americans, shrieking louder than needed in an effort to make some
meaning in the strange English language. A good man, who
stopped to talk as well as to make a practical deal. I brought
him my miserable cans, bottles, cloth, wire scraps. He would
look kindly at me and sadly at my junk and say, "Well, Paul" —
he pronounced it Powl — "it ain't worth it, but I'll give you a
dime." That was a happy sound, a dime delivered in an Iowa
alley by a voice out of the little towns of eastern Poland. Every
week he enriched my life with the sound of his voice, warm but
hard to understand, and by the offer of a dime. On some humiliating days I only got a nickel. His grandchildren are all doing very well and speak in fine, hard, Iowa voices.

A large battered bell hung from the collar of the harness.
Mother always gave me a sugar lump when we heard the junk
man's cry in the summer air. The bell didn't ring much when
the old horse walked, but after he had taken the sugar lump he
would nod his head up and down in thanks. The bell (obviously bought as junk) clanged and shimmered. With my tiny
gift I had caused that sound, which filled our backyard and
made Mother look out the window and smile. I have had few
moments of greater illumination in seventy-two years of a
lyrical-bitter life than standing in a rutted dirt alley in a small
midwestern town listening to a beat-up bell expressing the
gratitude of a beat-up horse driven by a beat-up old man driving a wagonload of beat-up junk.

There was a fire station in the next block. It had a big brass
bell on the wall, which cried out an alarm with such power that
we could hear it in the house. Then came the fire truck with its
larger bell. Even if it drove off in a direction away from us we
could still hear it for blocks.

A blind old man with a pack on his back walked slowly down

our street every few months, back bent both with age and the pack. He sharpened knives and scissors and carried a hand bell announcing his arrival. Mother always found something for him to sharpen. There is no more touching sight than that of a blind man running a crippled finger along the edge of a knife more tenderly than the hand of a man who can see. Once he let me ring his bell. Instead of banging it hard, I shook it gently, and he said, "I can tell you're a good boy." I didn't often hear that sentence, and I loved him for it.

In those days many people kept pens of chickens in town. Roosters crowing woke us every morning. I miss that arrogant and macho sound threatening the hens that they were going to have a busy day. One of our neighbors even kept a cow in order to have the freshest milk. Her indignant moo when she was late being milked floated over the streets with a rich, cross sound like the bulb horns squeezed by hand on those early cars, complaining at the sight of two pedestrians crossing the street.

All of us knew the blow of a blacksmith's hammer on a glowing horseshoe and the eloquent profanity of the blacksmith when a horse kicked him. We could tell at a distance and without seeing the horse whether he was walking, trotting, or cantering by the beat of his hooves on the road. How many now hear the pounding of a horse on a wooden bridge, an echoing sound like no other? The steel runners of a sleigh or bobsled hiss on the snow, and when they hit a bare spot on the pavement they screech. Horses passing on a street would neigh cheerfully. One would shriek, "You're an old so-and-so." The second horse would cry back, "And you're another." I had this straight from a horse.

People swear at their cars today, but then we would talk to our horses and pat them. Every day we combed out their manes and tails and rubbed them down after each ride. Father taught me always to speak to a horse before I walked behind it so I wouldn't get kicked. He talked to each horse as he went into its stall with oats, corn, and hay—a different voice from the one he used to talk to (howl at?) us children and quite different from the one he used with Mother. He had another voice for the dog and one for the cat that would sit up and beg for a pancake like a dog. Talking to animals, the human voice becomes more animal-like.

The first sound I heard each winter morning was the clatter of iron furnace grates, as Father shook the night's ashes, followed by the rattle of coal scooped up and shoveled onto the ashes after they had been covered with corncobs.

There was a lot of iron noise in our lives: heavy stove lids lifted and dropped, the bang of the iron skillet on the stove. And of course the nuts we cracked on the old sadiron, with the metallic crash of the hammer.

We had an ancient grindstone in the backyard where Father sharpened axes, hatchets, chisels, the blade of our plane. The buzz of steel on stone and the creak of the wheel as Father steadily turned it with his feet were soothing sounds.

Speech had not yet become homogenized by radio and television. Many accents were used daily. Across the street were Danes, the other way there were Russian Jews, down the block Czechs, Germans, Irish, English. There was even a family from New England who spoke in a way very foreign-sounding to us — she would call the boy we knew as Chuck, "Chahles."

How many times a day do you hear a man yelling at a horse that has just stepped on his foot?

My ears have lost the glory of their hearing.

SIGHTS

Horses needed water. Horse troughs were scattered around Cedar Rapids, and I remember horses on hot days bending over and blowing air with a gurgling sound into the water before drinking. One of the great sights of my early years was watching a great gulp of water swelling down the whole length of a horse's throat. The best place for drinking was a tall metal fountain on 16th Street where 3rd Avenue and Grande Avenue met. It had a dolphin on each side diving toward the water so that a horse could delight his eyes as well as cool his stomach. It now rests in Bever Park where I used to hike as a kid, but now it is only an ornament and no horses drink. The dolphins still dive.

We had two horse-headed hitching posts, one on 5th Avenue and the other on 16th Street, each with an iron ring in its mouth. Father would tie up his horse, pulling a sleigh in winter or a buggy in summer or, on days of long trips, a bobsled in the snow. He never left a bit in a horse's mouth but always took off the bridle and put on a comfortable halter. He came home at noon, putting a feed bag over the horse's nose so it could also have its lunch. One of the fine sights was a hungry horse tossing its head to get the last few oats from the bottom. Where have all the feed bags gone? Buggy whips are still made for horse shows, but I haven't seen one of those tough canvas bags in years. A healthy sound I liked to hear was that of a horse's broad teeth grinding the grain. I would stand looking up and see myself reflected in its wide eye.

There was the cattle drive down 5th Avenue bringing beef animals in from east of Cedar Rapids. Mother made me stand on the porch for fear I would be trampled to death. They came by snorting, frightened of the city, tossing their horns, trampling the lawns, a furious animal force, leaving the pavement filthy with their droppings. I learned from them, as I watched their massive motion, the power of mass.

The drugstore next to the butcher shop had a long tobacco counter, for in those days men smoked cigars and not cigarettes. ("Cigarettes are for French women," Father said with contempt, puffing on a cheap, acrid cigar.) The lids of the boxes were the first art I ever saw—Harvester, Antonio y Cleopatra, she in a skimpy white gown with a majestic figure under it, seated on a throne. It seemed to me that the bliss on her face came from the rich smell of the cigars rather than the presence of her admirer. There were so many scantily clad women on those lids I believed that tobacco was indeed, as my mother told me fearfully, a part of human sin. As to sin, I was shamefully eager, but too young to commit it. I loved the combination of racehorses and women—the two most beautiful shapes in the world.

On autumn evenings there were leaf fires as far as I could see along the street, with ghostly figures hovering around them. The night glowed. We would challenge each other to run through the dying fires. Nowadays when I see the bankers, lawyers, doctors who were my friends then, I can see them leaping through the smoke and flames. Now city governments stop this great October ritual in the name of clean air. I breathed deeply every year of that smoke and have no lung cancer.

One of the wonderful sights of those years was the variety of horse-drawn buggies, carts, wagons. Real craft went into them, a high skill in carving the dashboard of a sleigh with its swan-like curve. Bigger sleighs often had scenes painted on the sides; sometimes flowers and green trees slid cheerfully through the snow. There were endless styles of surreys, with their fringes shaking as the horse trotted. There were buggies with side curtains to protect them from rain and snow; the Amish in Iowa still use buggies, tying them up alongside cars, pickups, trucks at horse auctions. There were carts of all kinds, light, fast, often with red spokes flashing in the sun. How dull an auto tire seems compared to that. Wagons with tough oak sides hauled coal, sand, dirt, crushed stone, hay, straw, corn, oats, vegetables, and people, usually with a team of horses. The intricate leather harness was a joy to look at and to touch, the heavy tugs of the wagon, the light reins on the bit in the mouth, the bellyband, the curving collar with its brass tips on top (which I had to polish), the noseband which often had inlays of many colors, the crupper which fit under the tail and had to be cleaned often by me at age ten, the martingale which was fixed to the bellyband and ran up the chest of the horse and was fastened onto the bridle to keep the horse from throwing its head up when driven (I have used them on saddle horses, too), the noseband, the sidecheek, the cheek strap. There were also blinkers, sometimes called blinders—pieces of leather on the side of each eye to keep especially skittish horses from seeing objects that might scare them. The breeching was a heavy strap, often two layers, running from the hame tug on one side at the stifle, around the rear of the horse and fastening to the hame tug on the other side. These parts of the harness were graceful to look at, shone brightly if kept polished and rubbed with neat's-foot oil (I must have rubbed miles and miles as a kid), and smelled like a new pair of shoes.

We piled green-hulled black walnuts on the roof over our kitchen and waited until they turned soft and black. Then we shucked them in the backyard until our hands were stained dark brown for days. We had collected them by going into the woods and throwing sticks up into the branches, watching the swarms of heavy nuts falling around us.

Horse blankets in winter were every color and style. Mother used to sew them from used army blankets, pushing the thick fabric under the needle as her feet worked the treadle which turned the wheel; hands, eyes, feet were all busy at once. Some blankets were gray, some brown, some had stripes. There were fancy blankets to be bought in many colors and designs. The day we first put on the blankets the barn changed from a place of horses with coats of chestnut, white, gray, sorrel, and brown to rows of drab wool. They were tough to sew. Mother was tough.

Father had a long overcoat and long mittens made from the hide of a favorite horse that had died, and I had a small outfit, the warmest clothes I ever wore. In our matching outfits we went to horse sales, feed stores, farms, riding the sleigh with its brilliant bells or the bobsled with its heavy runners. There were white spots in odd places, and we must have looked curious in them, but I was proud of mine, for no other kid had such a coat. I knew the horse Father's outfit came from but was uneasy about the source of mine. Could it have been that spotted pony I used to ride, which had disappeared without explanation a year ago? I tried not to think of that. Father didn't say.

The family farm where Mother had been born, later farmed by Uncle Charlie, was on a hill in a grove of oak trees, the fields sloping down in all directions, the soil light and sandy, wonderful for watermelons, squash, pumpkins, but not good enough to raise the corn Charlie needed for his hogs and prize Jersey dairy cattle. At the northeast corner of the farm was a grove of tall hickory trees where we used to gather nuts for Aunt Gertrude's famous hickory-nut cake. Sometimes we would look out and see a fire of branches and shadows moving around the grove of trees. Charlie would say, "Looks like the Indians are back. Better not go down there, Paul." But I would go to the nearest point of the barnyard and look into the grove to watch them moving around and smell the hickory smoke of their fires, as sweet as the nuts from the trees. I was always told that hickory made the best Indian bows, tough but bending and springing back powerfully when pulled and released. I never saw any bows. "Probably sneaking into the cornfield for a few roasting ears," Charlie said. He didn't mind. With his generous heart he shared with the world what little he had, although he worked like a dog (how many dogs have you seen plowing a cornfield with a team of horses and a hand-held plow?) to get it. One morning they would be gone, and I would go to the grove to marvel at the still-warm ashes of their fires, the corncobs charred with flames (the Indians had really been in the field at night), watermelon rinds, scraps of cloth, once a tattered cornhusk doll. Looking back (my least favorite direction) I can see that it was all pathetic, the ruins of lives, but once I found a flint arrowhead, finely chipped, surely carried by one of the men as proof that he was descended from a once-powerful tribe that had hunted deer and other Indians and perhaps also whites, perhaps right in that grove and in that cornfield.

Gypsies also camped under those hickory trees, but where the Indians had been quiet, they were noisy and full of color. The Indians came in plain farm wagons, the Gypsies in brightly painted carts. The Indians slept on the ground, the Gypsies in their carts. At night we could hear the Gypsies singing, lively but mournful songs we could not understand. They had a lot of kids running around, their dress as colorful as their carts.

They were darker of skin than the Indians, more mysterious, for they seemed wholly foreign, while the Indians obviously belonged in that place and might have been returning to a campground of their ancestors. Charlie's cornfield and melon patch graciously contributed to the gypsy meals. One morning, after a night of singing and—judging by what we could see at a distance—dancing, they would be gone. No hickory nuts ever had the richness of those that came from the grove where ancient people had filled the air, which those trees breathed, with strange voices, songs in different languages and rhythms, hickory smoke enriched with the odor of corn and broiling meat, all of which seemed to have permeated the hard shells of the nuts.

Father had a cat that loved horses, and they loved her. My racehorse uncle used to keep a goat in the same stall with his most nervous pacer. If the goat was not there, the horse stamped and pawed, shook its head, whinnied. If these were quieter saddle horses, they still liked to have a small animal near them. Each autumn we put on those three- and five-gaited horses the warm blankets Mother had sewn, with pain because the cloth was too thick for her old sewing machine, so that the needle stabbed her fingers (there was blood on some blankets). Each autumn Saber had a litter of kittens (we called her that because she had very long teeth and I had read in a book about the saber-toothed tiger). She would march them up the boards on the side of a stall and jump onto the back of a horse, followed by four, five, six kittens. The heat from the horse's back went through the blanket and warmed that cat family. All winter it was the hottest bed in town. The kittens grew; their claws lengthened and sharpened.

In spring we took off the blankets. The first day Saber climbed up the stall and jumped on a horse with all of the kittens. For a few minutes all was peaceful. Then the horse would move, twitch its skin, and the cat family would dig in its claws. Suddenly the air would be full of flying cats as the horse bucked them off to get rid of those needle claws grabbing its hide. The cats always landed on their feet. From several stalls they would creep out, shaky but, in an animal way, unshaken. Father would set out a bowl of milk, and they would lap it up as if they were being rewarded for a glorious action. Next autumn Saber would be back on the blanket with a new litter.

Those sights have gone up in the hickory smoke. Now the grove has a concrete road lined with houses and at the end is a huge outdoor movie screen showing pornographic movies. They too have their shadowy figures seen at a distance by small boys forbidden to go there. Progress makes its fiery way, but my eyes have lost the glory of their seeing.

TASTES

In the winter, when it looked as if the kids in our family were getting "croupy," Mother would get out her bundle of sassafras bark from the roots of that plant and make us a hot, strong tea with a little sugar. It had an earthy taste, was a red-brown, and after two cups we began to sweat and then urinate. I haven't had a cup in a long time and assume I am the un-healthier for it.

Ham was a personal matter. When Charlie butchered on the farm, my cousins and I brought up dead branches from the hickory grove. The pig had been brought into his world of growing meat and sudden death by Charlie when the sow was farrowing; twice a day he had fed it skim milk, slops, oats, and ground corn, had watched it develop until it weighed two hundred pounds, then cut its throat into a big black pot, cut out the many parts, saved the tallow for lard, and sold the skin. (We believed it went into baseball mitts, and I don't want any-one to tell me it did not.) The hams were hung in the smoke-house, and all day we could hear the fat sizzling as it fell into the fire. The hams had no water added, no coloring, no preser-vatives. It was pure meat cured with pure and pungent smoke. I had scratched that pig's ears while it grunted, and I had felt the texture of those hams through those rough bristles and that tough hide many times. We had fed him, and now he was feed-ing us. It was a fair arrangement, save that it had a terminal effect on the pig. Our food was cooked in his lard, we ate his ribs barbecued, his chops, the sausage made from him, roasts. As Charlie said, "We're gonna use everything but the squeal, Paul, and I'm trying to figure out how to use that."

I used to help by turning the handle of the separator with cream running in a small stream out one spout and skim milk out the other, then set cans of both in the cold water of a tank in the milk house, taking a swig of each before it was cold. They still had the taste of an animal's body, lost when chilled. I also helped with the little churn for butter, revolving the handle as hard as I could. That fresh butter had nothing added but salt. I scraped the part stuck to the paddle, putting the last bit on my finger into my mouth. Shameful as it was, when no one was around I sometimes licked the paddle with my tongue to get the final flavor of that rich sweetness. Of course, the jams and preserves and pickles were all homemade. One of the great eating delights in the world, which the most expensive restaurant cannot offer, is to sit in a farm kitchen after a morning's work in the fields or barn, sit at a rough table with a slice of home-baked bread covered with newly churned butter topped with just-made strawberry or raspberry jam, and wash it down with fresh unpasteurized milk. Next to the elbow is the iron range on and in which these wonders had been prepared. It was massive, black, warm, part of the family. That hickory-smoked ham was baked in the range oven heated by a split-hickory fire. We heard the cooking fire snap and pop and watched the meat through an isinglass window in the oven door.

Eggs never came in a carton. Looking out the kitchen window, we could watch the hens, which had laid the eggs we were eating, chasing bugs, eating their feed, drinking gulps of water by tilting their heads far back, nourishing the next day's nourishing eggs. Like fresh milk, the taste of same-day eggs is wholly different from that of eggs sitting around a supermarket for days. A row of nests in a hen house, each with its fresh-laid egg, always brought to attention the nest that did not boast an egg. Then Charlie would look at the flock with a shrewd eye for the nonlaying hen, which had to be culled and cooked.

There is no flavor like that of homemade ice cream with real cream so thick it made the dasher hard to turn (I seem to have spent a remarkable amount of my childhood turning handles). I remember the handle getting harder and harder to turn, until I couldn't move it. Although we scraped the dasher, some ice cream always remained on it, and as with the butter I sneaked the chance to lick it; no ice cream in a cardboard carton that has been sitting in a freezer for weeks can come close in flavor to the scraps left on a dasher that your own tired arm has turned.

Breakfast was a savory affair, with the smoked sausage or ham tasting of hickory and nothing else, the egg laid an hour earlier, and the buckwheat pancakes covered with pure maple syrup and yesterday's home-churned butter. Buckwheat has a flavor wholly unlike white wheat, a brown, tangy, slightly sour taste, richer than wheat, strong as the smoky ham and sausage. Crepe suzettes—yuck!

Movie-theater popcorn has its place, but compared to popcorn prepared in a wire shaker over a wood fire, with the smack of smoke in it and fresh butter on it, it is bland stuff. You can watch the popping of the kernels you are about to eat. Then we would wash it down with apple juice or cider from the trees in the orchard that I had climbed in the summer. The taste of sunlight was in it.

Perhaps the greatest flavor was that of sweet corn—picked from the garden, five minutes in boiling water, ten minutes from stalk to mouth, with that same fresh butter. It is sweeter than chocolate, sweeter than ears traveling days by truck from Florida or Texas or resting on a store bin while its sugar disappears and what the customer tastes is starch. And again—that farm butter on it.

So with pickles—we could see from the window the garden where cucumbers grew before landing in a thick pot on the range and blending with the dill growing a few feet away. When we made mustard pickles (I say "we" because I was allowed to stand on a chair by the range with a towel around my waist for an apron and stir with a long wooden spoon), I had picked that mustard from the garden a few minutes before. No chemicals added, only herbs from our place; even the peppers for hot pickles grew before our eyes. No store-bought pickles have that crisp, fresh flavor.

The chicken, goose, duck, turkey were all friends we had helped grow to the right size. They didn't lie wrapped in cellophane for days, nor were they ever frozen, losing their basic "fowl" taste, which turns into that homogenized flavor so much food has today when it has been kept too long after slaughter. Save sausage, there was no processing, turning a meat into something different from the original.

Mother always made cornbread in the winter, and we ate it with the fresh butter that Charlie would drop off on his dairy route across Cedar Rapids, and with whatever syrup we had, maple, or sorghum, or Karo, or corn syrup. We had watched that corn grow. It had the flavor of late summer in it.

One special dish was sour beef, the pot roast cooked in vinegar, brought over from the "old country," southwest Germany. My small friends wouldn't touch it—they'd hold their noses—but I loved it and still do. Occasionally I find a restaurant with "sauerbraten," the closest thing.

No prepared mixes then. Mother made every cake, cookie, and pie from, literally, the bottom up, stirring them by hand in a heavy bowl with roses on the sides. I licked the batter from the spoon, as I had licked butter and ice cream; it had a quick sweetness. My tongue must have been the fastest in the west.

Now my tongue has lost the glory of its tasting.

It was a more physical world. We saw animals breeding and giving birth. We knew touches like the surprising softness of a horse's nose. When Father brought filthy horse blankets home, Mother washed them herself in the basement, by hand, without complaint. After they had soaked a few hours in boiling water and suds, the stench rose up and filled the house. Today we don't see the blind scissor-grinder—he is in a nursing home deteriorating because he is not out walking in all weathers; he is inside feeling useless. We do not hear his white stick tapping or his bell ringing. We see no more horses rearing on the street at the sound of a car horn or a train whistle. We do not see the white clabber hung in cloth bags from the ceiling of the root cellar, to be taken out so that rennet (from the stomach of a calf) can be added to make something similar to cottage cheese, but with a tangier taste. It is not easy for a man to have his foot run over by his own car, but in those days we were always getting stepped on by our horses; this was usually followed by an outraged voice invoking the name of the deity and commenting on the horse's ancestry. We gain in comfort and we lose our senses.

The Horse and I

The Engle family dragged the twentieth century kicking and screaming back into the nineteenth.

"Kicking" is the exact word, for we lived in the world of the horse. Our feet were stamped on by those heavy hooves, our shins were kicked, our fingers bitten; we were thrown from their backs. We almost died under them when they went down.

Yet horses and family were friends in a hard but marvelous relationship. Every morning and evening they had to be fed corn, oats, hay, water. If we were late, they pounded the floor like outraged diners in a poor restaurant. In the worst of the Depression, we ate what they ate — oatmeal, cornbread, water. Looking back, I can see that it was the thought of those huge, unfilled, hungry horse guts that drove Father to walk through snow, in the blackness before sunrise, a round trip of four miles, to feed them, and again in the evening. In return for their grain, they worked for us. Every dime (there weren't many) our father brought home came from renting them out to riders or from selling them. It was a total and mutual dependency. If we failed them, they starved. If they failed us, we starved. It was beautiful.

Ours was a horse house. Every autumn my tall and husky brother Bob and I piled fresh horse manure two feet deep around the foundation to keep the cold out of the basement. When Father came home, he took off his manurey boots in an entryway and hung his barn-smelling jacket in a kitchen alcove. Every autumn, we rubbed the harnesses, bridles, and saddles with neat's-foot oil. Added to the brownish smell of the barn, it gave the air in every room a sharp, crisp tang. Other houses in the neighborhood where I went to play with the kids surprised me — they had no scent at all, or only the revolting hints of starch, soap, furniture polish, the enemies of any boy whose lungs, like mine, had been enriched with the strong fragrance of horse manure and leather, as nourishing as bread, the odor of life.

In my earliest years, Father had work horses as well as saddle horses, but as a youth he had driven harness horses, trotters and pacers, at county fairs in Iowa. His proudest photographs were of himself holding a horse with one hand and in the other the blue, red, white, green, or yellow ribbon it had won. His first full job was buying, training, and selling coach horses. He had a "breaking cart" to which he would harness a half-trained horse. The cart had a step behind and a railing on top of the seat where my father sat holding the reins and whip. I would stand on the back step while we drove to the sandy, unpaved streets of Oak Hill above the Cedar River. There he would drive the green horse ("green" was his word for an ignorant horse or human) back and forth all morning, the sand slowing down the cart and tiring the horse so that he soon accepted the harsh bit in his mouth (a "curb" bit of solid steel, not the easier "snaffle" bit that swiveled in the middle) and the heavy harness on his back. But sometimes with a new horse there would be a fight all the way. The streets were lined with small houses with big families. Dogs rolled in the warm sand, chickens shook their feathers into it, cats used it for their nasty business, kids fought and fell in it until their hair and eyes were full of sand and even their howls of pain and anger had a sandy sound. The horse would send its muscle tension along the reins to Father's hands, and he would shout, "Hang on, Paul, he's gonna go!"

The horse rose up on its hind legs with a great, challenging whinny and took off down the road, the cart bouncing and swaying, sand flying from hooves and wheels, with me being thrown up but always hanging on and coming down, Father shouting at the horse and at the kids, dogs, and hens scattering ahead, yelling, mothers flying off porches and grabbing any moving object. And all the time Father heading the horse he could not stop toward a steep hill where the deep ruts would tire those powerful legs and my father's arms, thin but iron-tough, could finally slow the furious animal to a walk. The kids on the street loved it, the mothers hated it, and I both hated and loved it. Flying the Pacific Ocean nonstop San Francisco to Hong Kong is boring travel compared to that step on the breaking cart. Thirty-five thousand feet above sea level in a smooth jet plane is stupid when you can have a wild, flying, life-dangerous ride behind a cart that is half the time in the air and half the time on the ground, drawn by a beautiful creature that is half the time in the air and half the time on the ground.

When Father had collected one cattle car of horses, he would take them to New York city to auction off in a sales barn at the upper end of Times Square. He was shattered when I went to New York in the early thirties and told him that the barn was gone; there was only a jazz outfit called the Cotton Club in its place. But he had driven his horses on the "Harlem River Speedway" to show off their leg action, their high stepping, their solid bones to what he called the "New York swells" with their diamond pins in their cravats (his emphasis was on the first syllable, so that it rhymed with "rabbits"), their money green in their hands, no checks accepted.

At one end of the cattle car with Father's horses was the cot where he slept, next to his animals, watering and feeding them when the train pulled off on a siding. To the day he died, he talked about the places he traveled through when he was a young man, as if he had been an explorer in a wilderness. When I was first going to New York to be a graduate student at Columbia University, he gave me, along with advice about women ("Stay away, they'll pick your pocket"), a list of useful addresses. I was probably the first student of Renaissance English literature who was really prepared to understand the horse problems of Chaucer's *Canterbury Tales*. I, too, had ridden over green hills on winding roads, although my pilgrimage was only to a creek below the Cedar Rapids Country Club, where I would find golf balls floating down from the fairways and could sell them for a quarter. In all those books I read, no one mentioned that horses had to be shod, fed, rested, and watered, but when I read about the sweet showers of April in England, I heard the bridles clinking and the creak of saddle leather south of London. My father's New York city address list would have been invaluable in the 1890s. It was all feed

stores, harness shops, cheap restaurants, streets best for exer-
cising horses.

Father rented by the month two especially equipped wagons
and two horses to the telephone company. The wagons had
holders for pots of molten lead, racks for ladders, spindles for
coils of copper wire covered with heavy waxed paper, trunks
for tools and climbing irons. Each morning I would leave for
our barn at 6 A.M. to help harness up the horses. Then I would
drive two miles across town, holding the reins of the lead horse
in my left hand and the reins of the following horse in my right
hand, to the alley behind the telephone building, where I
would tie them to their wire-wrapped poles. I could tie a knot
that would never come loose, no matter how much throwing
of head and jerking of shoulders there was. Father always gave
me one piece of instruction as I was leaving: "To hell with what
happens. Just hang on, don't let go." The horses were well
trained, didn't even mind cars, but there was one moment of
terror on each trip. Ten railroad tracks ran through the center
of Cedar Rapids, not only main lines but also several tracks
used for switching cars among the Quaker Oats and other
plants. Moving trains did not bother the horses, but if an engine blew its whistle they both reared up and plunged to run
away, and when that happened—about once a week—I hung
on, howling at them, scared out of my skin, more afraid of
what Father would yell at me (and of the flat of his tough hand
on my bottom) than of going under the wheels of the wagons
or a train. I never let go, but there were days when my arms
ached from the pull of the horses and the bite of the reins
wrapped around my small fist. I screamed at the horses; I stood
up and sawed at the bits with both hands. I wept, not out of the
fear of pain but from fear of Father. But I never let go.

After tying up the wagons in the alley, I walked back across
the railroad tracks, marveling at how quiet they were, how
peaceful the air was after my fight with the horses. Old Washington High School was near the tracks. I arrived in time for
my first class, the only kid in school with trembling hands (and
sometimes mouth), with arm sockets aching so that it hurt to

turn a page in a book. Yet that book was Virgil's *Aeneid*; its ancient adventures were more fascinating than my own reckless chance with the horses half an hour earlier. Next day I took the wagons once again across the tracks. Once again I didn't let go.

Those horses were people to us. I suppose we were horses to them. Billy was a pinto, a black-and-white-spotted pony the size of a quarter horse. One flank had a black area the shape of Texas. He hated to be ridden and would shift nervously and quiver, pretending to be sick, when we hung a saddle by his stall. Father would shake a bridle behind Billy so that the curb chain clashed on the bit. Billy would break out in a sweat, as if he had already been ridden a hard mile on a hot day. He would fight having the bit put in his mouth, clenching his big white teeth and rubbing them together with a wicked grinding sound. Father had taught me how to pinch the inside corner of a horse's lips against his teeth so the pain would make him open his mouth and I could slip in the bit before he knew it was there. Billy was also a "sweller." When I threw the saddle on him, he would take a long breath and hold it, belly swollen, hoping that I would take up the cinch tight; when I turned away, he would let the air out of his lungs, his barrel would shrink, and then the cinch would be loose and easy. But I knew his tricks and would stand by his head until he simply had to breathe. He knew when he was beaten and would turn his big oval eyes, in which I could see my own reflection, to look at me with a bitter, betrayed, and (I swear it) affectionate and amused stare.

King was our favorite horse, a black, handsome, five-gaited gelding. He had all the gaits: walk, trot, canter, slow gait or single-foot, and rack. He had been shown in the ring and had won ribbons. I could take him out on our cinder ring in the wide area by the barn and put him into a rocking canter so slow and tight that he could keep a circle hardly wider than his own length, "turn on a dime" as Father said. Today he might say "on a dollar," but dime was more our medium of money, and besides, it better described the precision of his hooves in their dancing movement and the smallness of the circle. I would take King out in winter, the wind howling down from Canada, the snow fine underfoot, the speed of his rack making my hands and face ache with cold. King was so well trained and so intelligent that I could put him on a gait, place my mittened hands under my thigh and over the saddle for warmth, and let him go down the country road with no control over the bit. He never broke a gait. Yet he had a very soft mouth. Father would ride a horse he thought of buying and after one trip around the ring bring it back, get off, and say with contempt, "No. Hard mouth." He taught me to ride as much with voice as hands, telling the horse what was wanted instead of using force on the bit, quieting him down by the tone of talking when he was nervous, keeping soft those crucial inside curves of its mouth.

I was probably twelve years old when I first rode King, learning the difficult changes from all of the gaits, finding out how, once he hit a gait, to keep him from changing over to another, and especially how to get him off either on a right lead or a left lead for a canter and sensing when he might be going to shift from one to the other, how to prevent it by pressing gently on the left or the right side of the bit while calling to him in a singsong voice more chant than talk, watching the twitch of his ears as he heard and responded. If I leaned a little forward and to the left in the saddle, with a slight tug on the left rein, King would swing off in a left lead, rocking-chair canter.

King was a solid gleaming black, with a white blaze on his forehead and four white socks on his legs which flashed as he strode off with a high knee action, hocks bent and lifted. He trotted "square," hooves coming down directly ahead of his shoulders and not splaying out to the side, but his trot was his slowest gait. One day a buyer came from Chicago, red-faced, tall, loudmouthed, wearing a vest covered with many different breeds of multicolored horses like a sun rising over the horizon of his paunch, his hands fat and stubby. I looked at Father, he looked at me, and we shook our heads slightly. When we went into the barn to saddle King, Father whispered to me, "Now remember, his trot's bad. Push him on it, bring him along faster than he can move." We didn't like the looks of the buyer, but we needed folding money.

I talked to King and urged him to prance out like a circus horse with plumes. He stepped down the ring, lifting his legs as if the cinders still had their original fire and were burning. To prove how well trained he was, I took all four reins in my left hand (two for the hinged snaffle bit, two for the curb with its chain under his mouth—a strong pressure on the chain hurt the soft skin, but on King we never used it) to show off his responsiveness. Then the slow gait as in a horse show, my weight not shifting in the saddle. The canter was best, around the ring at a good clip, then slowing him down with that old horseman's secret prayer to the animal, a low, rhythmical "Whoo—oo, who—oo," quieter on the second syllable, as we came to the broad area of the ring. There I began to turn him in those close-coupled circles, still with one hand on the reins, in a motion so tight his hind hooves came down just where his front hooves had been. He held his gait as if he could go on all day.

Father called to me. I brought King up to the buyer at the same collected canter. When I stopped him he at once stretched out full length, head high, ears erect, not even champing the bits. "That's quite a horse you've got there, kid," the buyer said, walking around, looking beneath King for windpuffs or whitlows, or any swelling on the pasterns, and finding none, because King had never been abused. Then he looked at my father and said, "Looks like about eight hundred dollars' worth of horse to me," putting both thumbs in the tiny pockets of his vest, each with a horse on it, a cigar angled upward in his mouth, drawing smoke in and puffing it out while not touching it. Father glanced at me. It was two hundred more than he had hoped to get. "But I ain't seen him trot yet. Take him around, boy, let's see 'im move." Father jerked his head.

We started off at a slow clip.

I knew King better than I knew my nearby cousins or my older brother, who had left home young to take a job. I spent hours a week with him, talking, rubbing him down, feeding him almost as you feed a child. He would nuzzle me when I went into his stall on the left side (the same side you always mount a horse), giving him a couple of sugar cubes after each ride. He ate them with a hard grinding of his powerful white teeth, shaking his head for thanks in his expressive horse language.

I took him around two laps on the rack, that steady gait in which the body remains upright and does not move with the horse's moving, for in it the two legs on one side come down together and then the two on the other side, so that the horse's back remains flat.

I wanted King to do well. I couldn't bear to think of his leaving, of his soft mouth jerked by a strange hand, of being ridden by someone who did not even know that King understood English and responded to gentleness more than to harshness.

Heavy in heart, I stopped him (Father taught me always to come to a dead stop before changing to another gait) at the head of the ring. Then I leaned forward a little, eased off all pressure on the bits, put my right hand, not noticed by the buyer, on his mane and tugged it quickly while whispering to those glossy, listening ears, "Trot, King, trot." He strode off at a good but not spectacular gait. At the turn in the lower end of the ring I leaned forward again, called out, "Faster King, you've got to move," knocked on his right shoulder, urged him back toward the barn faster than he had ever trotted.

It was October. There were apple trees bordering the ring, and some apples had fallen on the cinders. King stepped on an apple and stumbled. Had he not been overextended it wouldn't have troubled him, but he was stretched out so far his legs were a little uncertain. He went half down, I flying over his head, King taking a final stride and then stopping by his great animal instinct, my head an inch from his right rear hoof with its steel shoe, which would have crushed my skull had he moved that one inch. King trembled and snorted but did not move. I crawled out from under him, my riding breeches torn, face scraped and bleeding, both elbows torn open and cinders black in the wounds. Father came running over. I waited for him to yell, to strike me.

The buyer walked over and looked at me in disgust. "I'm a big man," he sneered, rolling his cigar back and forth in his mouth while blowing the smoke out his nose. "I've got to have me a sure-footed animal." Our eight hundred dollars drove off down the ring in a white Apperson (do I remember accurately that it was called a Rabbit?). I waited for Father's blow, his reaction whenever I made a mistake.

He went over King with his hands to check for soundness, then he said to me in a voice softer than he had ever used before, "You okay, Paul? Can you walk? Any hurt bones?"

I shook my head to say no, tears more of failure than pain mingling with the blood and cinders on my face.

"Then get back on," he said firmly, "if you don't ride him right away, it's bad for the horse."

I understood at once. It was our family's system of values — what was good or bad for a horse was good or bad for us. When he got sick (seldom) Father took horse medicine, half a dose for himself, including a black, heavy, loud-smelling liquid called "Harlem Oil." It was his winter tonic.

King trembled still, but stretched out, head and ears up, the good, proud horse. I mounted, weeping, my bottom hurting in the saddle from the torn skin with cinders in it. Against pain and in King's honor I put him into a trot. My posting along with King's trot meant regular bangings against the saddle, which further beat up my bleeding bottom. I went around the ring three times until I had to stop or fall out of the saddle.

At the barn I pulled King up and got off. Father led him into the barn, saying to me, "You better wash that stuff off; I'll rub King down."

King and I spoke to each other every day, we touched each other, he carried me on his back gladly. Father did not believe in showing emotion unless it was overwhelming, and then he would break down and weep like a child. I knew he still owed money for the last load of good timothy hay. He needed that eight hundred dollars. Mother needed some of it to buy groceries for us in her frugal way. She would buy a bunch of carrots not only with care but with love. There were nights when the horses got the best ears of corn and the family had a wash basin of popcorn for supper.

Finally Father spoke. "You're a pretty good rider, Paul. Get a new pair of pants. I didn't want to sell King to that bastard anyway."

I still have those cinders in my elbows inside the scars.

I only saw Father go off an animal once. It was not a full horse but an oversized Shetland pony he had bought in Wyoming. At the age of ten I thought he meant that state of the high-pointed peaks so accurately called by the French (with homesick romanticism) the "Tetons" (tits). Then I discovered that our pony, called "Star" because of the white design on his black head, had really come from the small, pleasant farming town of Wyoming, east of Cedar Rapids. I am ashamed to admit that our Shetland was less impressive to me when I knew that he had come not out of snow-shining mountains but out of the same cornfield landscape, rolling, not flat, but without heights, that had also produced me (with the help of my parents).

Father's policy was the same as that of all horsemen: any four-legged creature was for sale at the right price. "Right" meant a little more than the animal was actually worth. I had ridden that Wyoming wild one without any trouble, with a small horn saddle, but Father wanted to impress a man looking for a safe pony to give his daughter. (In my male-chauvinist opinion, that ten-year-old girl was a spoiled brat with a pretty, sullen face, blue ribbons in her pigtails, a pug nose that wrinkled at the smell of a horse barn, and a whining voice that made a horse's whinny sound lyrical.) To prove what a gentle pony it was, Father put on the bridle and then jumped on its back without a saddle, shuffling down the cinder ring slowly. Coming back toward the barn he urged the Shetland along with a heel in its ribs. Startled and mad, the pony reared up on its hind legs, and Father slipped off its rump onto the cinders. As he lay there a moment, I knew clearly what was in his mind—whether to take a two-by-four and beat a little sense and courtesy into the Shetland named Star until he saw stars or to make it look like a proof of the little animal's quiet behavior. I ran over and took the reins while Father picked himself up with the ease of a fallen angel and said, "See, look how gentle. He didn't even kick."

Later in the barn, he said to me, in one of the few self-criticisms I ever heard him make, "Paul, it's one thing to take a chance and it's another to make a God-damn fool out of yourself." At ten, you don't answer that one.

The great horse experience of my childhood was the blacksmith shop. I would ride one horse and lead another down the long tree-gentled streets of Cedar Rapids, across those same reckless railroad tracks, often hanging on to a rearing horse with each hand if an engine blew its steam whistle. The blacksmith shop, at the edge of the Cedar River, was run by a Bohemian named Frank. He was twice the size of my father, with an accent as hard as the steel out of which he beat his horseshoes.

After tying the horses to rings in the wall and taking off the saddles (the bridles had already been replaced with strong halters), I would tell Frank what we wanted. "Toe weights on Buck's front feet," I would say, "and light heel weights on Jack." Frank knew as much as Father did about horses—never walk right up to the head of a horse without speaking. Let it know you are coming. Slap a hand on its rump, speak its name softly and clearly, run your hand along its flanks, treat it like a woman (those tough guys were subtler than you would believe if you just looked at their jaw, their strong arms, their penetrating eyes), then give it a final pat on the head and talk, talk, talk, it didn't matter what you said, just keep your human voice reverberating in its ear.

Frank's native language was Czech. Next to those kicking and dangerous horses, what he said to them in his own speech seemed far more eloquent and tougher than our flat English. Sometimes when Frank was turning the fan of the forge with one hand and holding the horseshoe in the glowing coal with tongs in the other hand, he would lift the shoe out of the fire and hold it in the air glowing like a star, take a swig from a bottle of homemade wine (it was Prohibition time, but the cheerful Czechs made their own wine from backyard grapes in the immaculate gardens they all had; a lot of the local police were Czech, and a change in an obscure and obviously absurd American law had not changed their thirst), spit on the shoe, watch it sizzle, then plunge it back for a final heating before he beat it on the forge. This was the mysterious secret, revealing why the Engle horses were the highest steppers in Cedar Rapids — they had wine in their shoes.

Some horses accept the nails in their hooves as a natural part of being a horse. Some cannot take the single pound of the hammer without kicking. When I took a horse that was frightened not only of having its hoof clipped and shaved by a file but also of the smell of burning hoof, of the roar of the bellows and the stench of the coal, Frank would say quietly, "Paul, we better put the twitch on." I hated that. The twitch was a three-foot length of seasoned oak with a hole in one end through which a rawhide string had been tied. My job was to grab the horse's upper lip, shove it through the rawhide loop, then twist the oak until it completely held the sensitive lip in the rawhide thong. I never knew a horse, however frightened of the clippers on the bones of his head or of the first set of shoes pounded on his hooves, to jump when the twitch was on it. Sometimes Frank could feel the horse's muscles beginning to tighten, and he would yell, "Give that sonabitchin' twitch another half twist, Paul." As I turned the oak pole I saw the horse lay back its ears, roll its eyes, scared by the sudden pain. It would tremble, but not jump, not throw its head. I trembled too, for hanging on hard to the twitch also twisted my small arms, and I was afraid the twitch would slip off. It did, once, when I hadn't turned it quite enough, and there was all hell to pay — the horse kicked out with its hind legs, and Frank blasted through the air and into the opposite wall of the blacksmith shop, the tongs and horseshoe striking the forge with a steely clang. The tossing of its head threw me against the wall to which it was tied, and I went down on the floor by its front feet, still hanging on to the twitch.

When Frank was mad he swore in Czech, the most eloquent and outraged sounds I have ever heard, compared to which profanity in English sounds like a Sunday school prayer. There was one advantage: I couldn't tell if he was cussing me or the horse. Probably both.

The horse stamped on the plank floor, shaking its head and wriggling its sore upper lip. Frank looked at me grimly, rubbing his sore hip, took a swig of wine, and said, "You hung on, Paul, you hung on. Now we gotta do it again or that bastard won't ever get shod, once he's got the idea he can get away with it."

I stood up, clutching the twitch, and waited in terror while Frank grabbed the lip and again twisted the rawhide loop, this time until the oak was hard against the horse's upper jaw. Then he handed it to me, picked up horseshoe and tongs, heated the shoe again in the forge, spat his wine spit on the steel to test its temper, backed up to the horse, grabbed the same leg between his own legs, put nails in his mouth, and took a hammer in that massive fist at the end of a muscular arm; and in two minutes the job was done. I was so weak from fright and from hanging on (Father had beaten into me the notion that mankind was put into this dirty world to hang on) that I could hardly untwist the loop.

Frank muttered, trying to hide the fact that he wanted to say something kind to me, "You did your best. I won't tell your old man."

I was hardly able to walk, and yet I had to bridle and saddle those tense horses and ride several miles across Cedar Rapids. It seemed like a normal day in a boy's life. I didn't know it then, but it was a great way to prepare for poetry and teaching.

Father had a blood feud with the automobile, which had caused the streets of Cedar Rapids to be paved. It was a menace to the legs of horses and a danger in winter when they iced over and even "sharp-shod" horses slipped. When he finally gave in and bought an old touring car, he drove it through the end of the garage (which he had built reluctantly in our backyard where the hen coop had stood), shouting, as the wood fell on the cloth roof of the car, "Whoa, God damn it, whoa, or I'll beat some sense into you."

Mother's life was a long martyrdom to the smell, sound, and talk of horses. She hated the profane language of horsemen, the ammonia stench of urine in their clothes, the violence of breaking horses and the breaking of human bones that went with it. She dreaded that one of us children would want to be in the horse business. But when Father brought me home after the fall from King, she bathed my skin, poured on some foaming medicine which burned the bleeding flesh, made no complaint, laughed when she looked at me, and said, "You're the dirtiest kid I ever saw." She even asked Father, "Is the horse all right?" It was our family speaking.

If indeed there is a heaven, I know how Father will enter it: smelling of the horse barn, riding King at a steady trot, watching to see that he did not stumble on clouds, crooning to him in horse language to keep his head high, his ears forward, his hocks snapping sharply; the saddle leather creaking as Father posted (surely it was the same saddle I had polished the winter before until it glowed and turned supple to the touch). And King would whinny back at the angelic choirs as he trotted straight and true and a little faster than he had ever trotted before.

I was a lucky kid, living close to those tall and beautiful animals at the beginning of the auto age, before the horsepower of internal-combustion engines replaced the horse. No stink is worse than inhaled gasoline fumes; no smell was healthier than a horse barn's blended odor of hay, straw, oats, leather, horse manure. Nothing in any car is as deep, alive, liquid-looking as the oval eye of a horse with your face reflected in it. I knew animal life. I pity the young today who do not know it. Understanding those great creatures, helping them when they were ill or hurt (in spite of their strength, horses are very vulnerable to diseases, muscle tears, bone injuries), depending on them to take us across town or out into the country, we understood better the hazards and joys of our own reckless lives on this restless earth.

Those Damn Jews

My life among Jews began at a fiery furnace when I was a kid of ten in that pleasant city of Cedar Rapids, Iowa, and continued at the fireless furnaces of Auschwitz.

It all began on a morning when our neighbor, who worked at a filling station and walked with a gait which my horse-handling father called "gimpy," stopped at our house and said bitterly, pointing down the street, "Those damn Jews have moved in." I had never known that word and assumed those people would have a different color or shape from us; in any case, I thought, avoid them. Our neighbor, thin, nervous, with huge hands dangling from his wrists like untamed animals (his harsh eyes showed that he used them to beat his wife and children), moved on to his day of gas and tires, leaving me in fear.

A week later I met a daughter of the Jewish family in our neighborhood drugstore. To my amazement, she looked like my aunt Effie the quick-moving, who always shook her long black hair when she talked. The daughter seemed quite old to me, although, looking back, I think she must have been in her twenties. She spoke kindly to me, with an accent I had never heard, so different from our solid midwestern pronunciation; we believed that God had put the letter "r" in the English alphabet so that it could be given an honest, haarrd sound. I moved away from her, still scared.

A few days later she stopped me on the street, saying, "My name is Reba Goldstein. Do you want to earn some money?" I could not speak; I looked for the quickest way to run home. She went on, "You come to our house Saturday morning. Light fires. Fifteen cents."

It was a tough decision. I was frightened of that house. I needed fifteen cents. Reba was no beauty, but when she smiled the very bones of her face seemed to soften. She was so eager to have me say "Yes" that she leaned toward me and held out her hands. I leaned back, afraid that she would touch me with those Jewish fingers, those damn fingers. Then Reba said gently, "Paul, we need you. In our religion we cannot make fire on Saturdays, because it is our holy day."

I knew about holiness, having never missed a Sunday school class since I started at four years. But if Jews were also religious, how could our neighbor with the grease-grimy shirt use the word "damn" about them? And my Methodist church admitted that Christ was a Jew. On that sidewalk, the late autumn sun shimmering through a maple tree whose leaves had turned red, I trembled in the first moral dilemma of my life.

Reba spoke again, "Paul, we need you." I had been staring down at my scruffy shoes as if they could of their own will walk me away from that moment of fear, embarrassment, and shame. I looked up at Reba. The smile on her plain face caressed me. What came from her eyes seemed not damn Jewishness but sunlight. More than Iowa maple leaves hovered in that tense air.

"Okay," I told her.

"Come at six-thirty Saturday morning. And thank you." Reba floated off toward her mysterious house. I ran home, and I didn't have the nerve to tell my mother.

So I got my first job. I became a shabbas goy, a non-Jew who did on the Jewish sabbath, our Saturday, the work which Exodus 35, Verse 3, ordered its people not to do: "Ye shall kindle no fire throughout your habitations upon the sabbath day." That ancient Hebraic law put fifteen cents in the pocket of a boy of "pure" German descent. How strange that my Black Forest shoemaking ancestors should have come to the United States and allowed me to lead a life of gas and fire among Jews. Sixty years later, standing by the dynamited gas chambers and rusting furnaces of Auschwitz, I had come full circle. I wept inside, not only for the millions destroyed in Europe but for my Jewish families back in Iowa, who had been burned not by fire but by the agonizing knowledge of what had happened to their people.

On the first Saturday morning in Cedar Rapids, that decent, tree-filled city, I knocked softly on the back door of the Goldstein house, ready to run from the horrors inside. Reba opened the door. Behind her was the grandfather, tall, heavily bearded, dressed in black, black-hatted, speaking to Reba in words that did not sound to me like a language but like blackness talking. My filling-station neighbor was right. I had come there at the risk of my life.

Reba led me up some steps to the kitchen. At the stove, I turned on the gas and lit it with a match, then put on the burners pots of food prepared the evening before. Grandfather gestured toward the stairs, and I followed him down to the basement, in panic but lusting for that fifteen cents, and confronted a furnace just like the one we had at home. Reba said, "First you shake it." I shook the grates until the night's ashes fell down and only the coals remained. Then Grandfather pointed to a dark room. I entered it, ready to fight or flee. He pointed to a pile of corncobs and a scoop shovel. Suddenly, great joy and peace came to me; I was back in my own element. The corncob was the central object of my life. I was an expert in that symmetrical art form so honored in the folklore of American life before modern plumbing.

Corncobs are the greatest fire-making tinder. Grandfather opened the furnace door and showed me just where to put my scoop of cobs at the back of the grate. There was wood kindling in the dark room, and I added some to the fire. Then I added coal, banking it so that the fire would burn slowly and last all morning. I adjusted the draft to low, and my early-morning work was done. The black voice spoke to Reba, who told me, "You'll be fine, he says. Come back at noon," and she patted my shoulder with those long Jewish fingers; they felt like the velvet of my mother's one good jacket.

I walked out into the glittering daylight from the dungeon of the cellar, a free man with an exuberant heart, a worker with a weekly income doing a useful job that had a vague religious shimmer over it. (I have forgotten the Yiddish for corncob — alas for the way time rots the memory.) That morning I played with my friends in an exalted state, my Methodist soul rejoicing that now I would be celebrating two sabbaths. And getting paid!

At noon I was back, turning out the burners on the gas stove and stoking the furnace again. Grandfather's hands danced as he dramatized in the air how I was to shape the cobs, the wood (very little needed at noon), and the coal so that the fire would last until, with darkness, he could do it himself.

As I opened the back door to leave, the fifteen cents shining in my hand, for how could I hide the coins away in my pocket, the old fear came back. Walking toward me from the alley where he had tied his horse to a telephone pole was the rabbi, a kosher chicken hanging from one hand, spotted with blood. I had been warned about rabbis by my gentile friends — they did terrible things with knives to boys. Without thinking, I turned and ran down to the cellar. But that rabbi in his long black coat and his strange hat followed me. I jumped into the coal room, now my salvation. The rabbi went over and put the chicken in an ice box, then came up to me, saying, "Are you Paul, the new shabbas goy? It's a good name, Paul," and went up the stairs.

Gradually my reputation as a loyal worker spread. Another Jewish family a block away hired me. Then the rabbi too, and my fortune was up to forty-five cents a week. Once the rabbi took me to the synagogue across the Cedar River, and I entered that mystery without fear.

My grandfather's name was Jacob Reinheimer. My Jewish grandfather's name, I found, was something which sounded like "Yacov," the same name. We began to talk to each other, he in Yiddish and I in English, so that soon each began to know a few phrases of the other's language. The rabbi taught me a few Hebrew words. I was the linguist on my block. Once when our filling-station neighbor walked by I yelled a Yiddish phrase at him. He stopped, stared at me with those cruel eyes, and said, "Paul, they're getting power over you. They killed Christ. You'll fry in hell." And he strode off to repair more inner tubes. I considered my fate for a moment, then decided that if Reba and Grandfather Yacov were with me in hell, it wouldn't be so bad.

I tended my fires for years. Sometimes on cold autumn days I would be playing pickup football on the school playground when Reba would appear on the sideline and wave to me. I understood. The gas fire on the stove had blown out. I would leave the game, often to howls from my team, "Come on, Paul, we got a first down, you can't go. Wanna carry the ball?" But I always got on my bike, started the flame again, and came back in time to have my teeth rattled or my nose broken. (It is still crooked from being kicked sideways; my neighbor who wrestled tires all day said it was proper punishment for my Jewish sins.)

Then I met the poet, out of a Jewish immigrant family from Vienna, son of a peddler of tin pots in the Ozark Mountains of southwestern Missouri, who drove over the tough hills (the "arcs") selling pans out of a buggy to the poor families clinging for their lives to those rocky slopes. His name was that of an angel, Gabriel, and he could be a devil. As a kid he spoke Yiddish and Osage and then learned English from Catholic sisters; his talk was full of Christian phrases and Ozark mountain talk, invocations of the saints and earthy references to the fact that men and women were really made out of the humble body of the earth. I was writing poetry and so was he; mine was about the usual glories and horrors of adolescence, his about the tough-minded, tough-muscled, tough-talking Ozark farmers. I had long since given up carrying the torch as a shabbas goy; he had long since given up his department-store life, after a massive heart attack. After hours at my drugstore job I would go to his apartment, where he lay on a couch in a robe, and intone my poems in what must have been a revolting cracked voice. Gabe would listen with (alleged) interest, and then say, "Now, Paul, I've got a new one," and he would read in that near-hillbilly accent a poem of violence and love and hate and hound dogs that would have shocked his Viennese ancestors.

The years rolled their brutal course down the hill of time. Still poor, my clothes still smelling of the horse barn, still writing those doubtful poems where too much emotion clashed with too many words, I went one evening to Gabe and told him that I had just been given a Rhodes Scholarship for three years at Oxford University. He looked at me with those strong and fiery eyes which lit up all of that weakened body. Silence while he handled the shock of my news. Then he said, quietly, "What clothes are you going to wear when you land in Oxford?"

I looked down at the cheap stuff I was wearing. "These."

Gabe's temper was like an owl — it was quick to take off, and it could fly through darkness. With the shout of an Old Testament prophet accusing a sinner, his small hands making large circles in the air, each of his eyes a burning bush, Gabe screamed at me, "No son of mine" — by then I had become an honorary son — "is going to go to England looking like that! Go down to the store tomorrow. I'll leave orders. Start from scratch. Get an outfit that won't make us ashamed. Jesus Christ, if you'll excuse my using that expression, you look like a bum. And now you're going to become a God-damn gentleman, the first one in your family." He paused for breath. Then he said with a great effort (he was not supposed to become excited, because of his failing heart), lifting his hands toward me with such a gesture of love as I have seldom known (or endured) in a life which has been lucky with those who have loved me for the person they innocently thought I really was, "Paul, I want you to start with a bare ass. Get everything." Across the room, his shaking hands seemed to touch my forehead. I could not read another poem. I could not speak.

Next morning I went to every department of Gabe's store. Socks, underwear, shirts, neckties, suits, overcoat, raincoat, hat. Looking back, I can see that one suit must have been a horror; it had not only trousers and jacket but also a revolting object called "golf knickers," emphasizing my naturally bowed legs. When I walked through the ancient dark gate of Merton College, Oxford, A.D. 1256, in a university which for centuries Jews had been forbidden to enter, I was wearing wholly Jewish clothes. There was one gentile feature — I had escaped the rabbi's knife.

For my Oxford degree I had to translate French and German philosophy (as it turned out, Descartes and Kant) at sight, without a dictionary. That meant Germany for my first summer vacation, to learn the thorny language on my own. Without grammar, phrase book, or dictionary I lived in the mountains of Bavaria. There I met Franz, the truest European I ever knew. He sang folk songs in French. He had taught at the school in Bishop Stortford in England which Cecil Rhodes, my diamond-gold benefactor, had attended. He left in July 1914 for a month at home in Germany and never returned, caught in the division of students that was later massacred at Lange-marck. He had written a Ph.D. dissertation on "Die Philoso-phie von als ob," the philosophy of as if. Nothing could have been more relevant to Nazi Germany of those years than the concept of reality not as existential being but "as if" what you experienced in your blind emotions was actually true.

Franz invited me to spend Christmas 1934 with his family in Berlin-Friedenau, one of the suburbs absorbed by that great stony capital. I haunted the bookstores, especially around von Kleist Platz. By then I could translate the rhythmical, image-loaded poems of Rainer Maria Rilke — a German from Prague, secretary to Rodin, isolated, made to wear girl's dresses until he went to military school, needing human com-panionship as a dog needs bones, yet frightened of intimacy and commitment. There was one shop I went to almost daily, for it had a shelf of Rilke books in a fine edition, bound in half-leather. I would take them down not to read but only to hold. It was like touching the skin of Rilke to feel that soft binding and the colored title pages. One day the old man who owned the store came up to me and asked, "Would you like a cup of tea?" The store was long and one-room wide; a corridor led along one wall, with small rooms off to the left, all of them crammed with old books. We carried all of the Rilke books with us. I assumed he was going to offer me a special discount if I bought all of them, but even that I could not afford. He showed me into a room with table and chairs. The Rilke books sat on the table between us like sacred objects brought back by a dangerous expedition from a long-sealed tomb. I could not touch them.

The old man called out toward a closed door. Soon tea was

brought in by an obviously very intelligent girl of sixteen, hair and eyes black as night, glowing, glowing. She bowed to me and fled. Pouring tea, the old man said gently, as if he were blessing a child, "I see you like Rilke. Take them. Take all of the books. They are too precious to sell."

Suddenly, they were mine, those loved poems written by that poet always in flight, in Worpswede, Paris, Switzerland, in a castle above the Adriatic, the poet who always had women looking after him but could not live with his wife, the poet Germans called "der weibliche Dichter," the feminine, or womanly, poet.

"Why?" I asked.

He stared at me the way an animal will look at a human being to whose hands he is entrusting his life. Total, no reservations, to the death. "I am a Jew."

He waved his hands toward all the rooms of books. "They will destroy all of this." (He never used the words for which "Nazi" is an abbreviation; they were always "they." But I knew, I knew, from the darkness in his voice.)

Then he turned and gestured toward the door the lovely girl had closed. "I am old. It does not matter. But my daughter, that girl." He could not speak, his throat muttered wordless sounds which were the most moving language I had ever heard. Again, I weep inside to recall it.

He turned his eyes toward me. They burned my eyes.

"She must go. Out of Germany. We are the damned Jews." (Old filling-station neighbor, you knew little of what you were saying. You would have looked at home in a Sturmabteilung uniform.)

"I know your name. It was on a traveler's check you gave me for some books. You are Paul. You are American. You are the lucky one. My daughter, Rebekah, get her out. Take her out. Leave me to die. We Jews are very skilled at dying. If you are in trouble, come to Jews. They know so much about it."

The room shrank to my body's size. For a moment, I was in a trap, its teeth on my neck. Outside, I heard the Nazi boots marching, the shouts in marching cadence, "Sieg Heil, Sieg

Heil," hail victory, hail victory. Victory over the helpless little man opposite me, his thin hands trembling, his head shaking, the tears of two thousand years falling down his cheeks, all his life flowing into his begging eyes. I was ashamed to sit, in my American security, in the same room with the whole nervous system of an old Jew dumped into my lap.

"I will try," I said stupidly, "I will try."

Rebekah entered the room. Standing close to me, she caressed my face with her eyes, said nothing, bowed with more dignity than I had ever seen in a human being, picked up the teapot as if it were a chalice on an altar, and backed out of the room, looking at me, looking at me, with trust, with trust, a flame which could miraculously walk across the floor and close the door.

Back home a month later, I found people who promised to help. I wrote the family. My letter was returned stamped "Verschwunden." *Disappeared.* Do not be patient with the frightfulness of the human race. Howl, howl. From your dark cave, howl.

It was Friday, and after dinner that evening Franz said, "Now Paul, tonight someone will come. We will go into that room." He pointed to a little odd room in the center of the apartment, the room without windows or outside walls. "Speak softly." All week such bits of food as would not spoil had been saved. Now they put it on the table.

"Who is coming?" I asked.

Franz whispered, "Die alte Judische Witwe" — the old Jewish widow. "She was my friend's wife. He was not Jewish. But she must eat."

It could be death for a German to do what Franz was doing.

There was a wide stairway up the front of the building and a narrow iron stairway at the back. We heard small steps on the iron. The kitchen door had been left unlocked. It opened softly. A tiny lady in black carrying an empty string bag came in and sat down without speaking. Franz went over and took her hands. There in Berlin, with all hell about to break across what has laughingly been called civilized Europe, a brave

German embraced a terrified Jew. I remember thinking in that moment, "Paul, you'd better go back to Iowa. You haven't the strength to be part of this appalling life. Go back to your safe and friendly Jews in the clothing store."

The widow suddenly saw me and put her hands over her eyes in fright. "Is he one of them?" she asked Franz.

He shook his head. "He is our American friend."

"America." She spoke the word as if it were the magical incantation that would open sealed doors and deliver you into heaven, which was, quite simply, a farming state called Iowa, which had no Nazi Party. "America, America." She rolled the word on her tongue as a child treasures a piece of candy, wanting it to last. She left with her scraps. At the door, as she stepped out into the ultimate dark pit of Berlin, she looked at me in disbelief and spoke to no one, only to her own anguished mind, "America."

Next morning I left Berlin. Lying in the gutter outside the apartment building was a dead man, hands bound behind with adhesive tape, ankles bound, a wide strip of tape across his mouth, one over his eyes. The Nazis had come again in the night. And dear Jewish widow, did you make it home with the remnants of our humble food?

On the way to the railroad station, the old Potsdamer Bahnhof, we passed a little store with its windows smashed. Hung on the door was a sign, "Deutschland wird Judenfrei" — Germany will be Jew-free. Franz took my hand, then shook his head in the ancient gesture meaning *No*. He dared not talk in the presence of the taxi driver. He knew it all. He was mourning the dead to come.

When I arrived in New York from my Oxford-and-Europe years (on a German ship, ironically, the *Bremen*, which I had boarded in Bremerhaven), I was waiting down in third class while a tug pulled us into the harbor. The purser came through, holding his nose at the degradation of slumming in that area so deep in the ship, so crammed with people obviously poor and obviously not too well bathed. He held up a letter in his right hand and called a name. Finally I realized that it was mine. He held it out to me carefully, so that his pure Aryan hand would not touch mine. He did not know that I was "pure Aryan" too.

The letter was from Gabe: "If you have come back from Europe without having spent every cent you had, you are no son of mine. Here are a few dollars. Don't spend them on anything sensible. Love." I had arrived without the money for a cab to take my luggage from the dock. All I had was a dime to call a friend and ask him to bring money so that I could go live with him a while in New York.

I wrote Gabe my address. Next week a telegram arrived with money for the fare to Florida and a message buried in his usual way of expressing affection: "Come on down and stew in your own Jews." I went. We wept. Tears that would cut stone, because I had seen the Jews of Germany stoned, and Gabe knew it.

By then I had discovered that Jews were indeed damned, but in ways my neighbor could not have imagined. I had found his kind, those who marched east to die in the snows west of Moscow (he would gladly have joined them) in honor of that pig with the little row of pig bristles on his upper lip. I knew about pigs, that noble animal so abundant in Iowa, and I apologize to them for the comparison.

In Krakow the night before I went to Auschwitz so many years and so many deaths later, a German-speaking Polish man had held out his hand toward me, asking, "Do you know what that is?"

"No, what is it?"

"That's a dead Jew."

Innocently, I asked, "But how do I know it is a dead Jew?"

"Because," he sneered, "if it was a live Jew it would be doing this." He rubbed his thumb back and forth across the palm of his hand, as if he were counting money.

Human life is too difficult for people.

At Auschwitz I stood on the caved-in gas chamber by the vent through which the canisters of "Zyklon" gas had been dropped into the room crowded with naked men, women, and children. I felt Grandfather's fleeing Poland, rabbi's pointing at things and speaking their Hebrew names, old Gabe's battling pain like a boxer, Reba, who hired me for a shabbas goy, the old man who loved Rilke's books, daughter Rebekah, whose eyes are on me as I write these inadequate words—I felt them walking toward me with their devoted but accusing eyes.

I was back with my own Jews. I was home. The railroad tracks that had carried those suffering people was just beyond the place where I stood. The thin whistle of a train on its way to Krakow. The dead crying.

The leaves of white birches trembled in the white sunlight. (The Nazis had called the place "Birkenau," the place of birches.) My feet sank into the concrete. I was too moved to move.

I was a lucky kid, living close to those remote people. They brought a strange, foreign quality into our modest midwestern neighborhood of small wooden houses where all families lived cheerfully together in the shared condition of hard work and little money. It was wonderful to be taken in as an honorary Jew by those whom I had at first feared. Nothing was better preparation for Hitler's Germany than to have worked as a maker of fires for a group so soon to be frozen out of the society in which it lived. Had I not known Reba and old Grandpa with his yarmulke and his Yiddish and Gabe with his fiery heart (and temper) and his cold hands, I would not have understood so well the faces and lives and the unbearable eyes of the Jewish widow and of the Rilke-loving Jewish bookseller in Berlin, eyes beyond bitterness, beyond suffering. They haunt me still. There are nights when I seem to find them staring at me through the window out of that blackness which is no different from that dark world they knew. They accuse me that I did so little for them. I admit my guilt. I can give them nothing but my lifelong love. If I could only touch their hands.

Remember Memorial Day?

The way we celebrated it, there was little gloomy about Memorial Day; everything we did was gay and life-giving. Early in the morning my sisters and I would be out cutting flowers, wrapping the stems in damp cloth. It was important that we took our own flowers to our own people. My brother would come out with his pocket knife, the big blade honed to an edge so sharp he would take a hair from my head and hold it up, and as he slashed at it like a scalping Indian he would shout proudly, "Couldn't feel it, could you?" Because he was tall, he would cut the lilacs with his knife, piling the blooms into my arms until their fragrance seemed as solid as the flowers themselves and the sprays reached as high as my head. I was allowed to gather some iris with the knife, and I can still hear the crisp, ripping sound as the blade severed the stalks.

By now my father would have driven up, with our favorite chestnut horse, Alice, hitched to the light wagon. Alice was one of those gracious ladies with whom the world is blessed: gentle-mannered, sturdy, fond of children. On her patient and shining back all of us learned to ride. We learned to post in the saddle on her smooth trot and to rock smoothly in her rocking-chair canter. Now she was gleaming for the holiday. After all, you can curry and brush a horse in a tenth of the time it takes to wash a car.

Into the wagon went our Memorial Day equipment: a lawn mower, a sickle, a picnic basket, all the bundles of flowers, a horse blanket for spreading on the ground while we ate. We four children sat in the back and our parents on the seat, my father trailing the lines behind him so that I could hang on to them and pretend to help drive.

Off we trotted in the bright sun, a wagonload of good smells, the fresh oat straw on which we sat, the flowers surrounding us with their mingled fragrances, the picnic basket with its smell of fresh home-baked bread, the tang of hot leather and the sweating horse.

We drove six miles to the small town where my mother's people were buried. The cemetery was on a long wooded hill, very gay with people moving around, all of them carrying armloads of flowers and baskets. My father took the lawn mower, my brother the sickle, and my sisters the flowers, while my mother and I shared the basket handles. There was a dense bush we called a snowball at the head of the plot, and thrushes had always nested there by the end of May, rushing out of the branches with an angry twittering when we approached, for after all it was their place the rest of the year.

My mother's father had been a Civil War veteran, and he had a little military marker with a tiny flag at his grave. We usually arrived just as the parade reached the cemetery, so that I could watch the few surviving veterans stand raggedly and proudly while a detail fired blanks into the air. I remembered my grandfather sniffing at the modern rifles, saying, "You ought to have heard those muskets we had. Didn't need to shoot a man. The sound would kill him."

It was a pleasant visit, with the tiny flags bright on the hill, the homegrown flowers adding their colors to all the shrubs in bloom, the slope full of the cheerful sound of whirring lawn mowers as families, under the old-fashioned custom long since changed, tended the graves themselves. There was only one moment of sadness for me: when I saw the short grave of the one brother in my mother's family who had died young, and for whom I had been named. On the first Memorial Day after I had turned nine—and was no longer scared of dying at eight, as he had—I came to his grave with a feeling both of relief at having lived beyond the fatal year and of sympathy for this uncle who from that time on would always be younger than I.

The graves now looking neat and the flowers arranged on them, we would load up the wagon and drive out into the country along a curving sandy road, where Alice would have to strain and the children would hop out and run alongside. We picked wildflowers, blue lupine, gentian, violets, wild roses to add to the tame ones from home. We had a spade in the wagon, and now and then would dig up an entire bush of wild roses for planting in the rural cemetery we were going to.

This was country where both Mother and Father had lived as children, and they remembered every place. It was almost a homecoming, as my father would point with his long whip and say, "Look at that, somebody must have bought the old Glass place." And my mother would look across the road and ask, with a light echo of homesickness in her gentle voice, "Remember when the Grieshabers moved in there? Couldn't speak a word of anything but German." And my father would reply, "There was an honest man. I never had to go out and smell his hay before I bought it."

So it was that this trip to the dead brought back to the living a heightened sense of their own lives. To the children, it gave an awareness of the ranging life behind them, of the very people who had made that road.

As a girl, Mother had walked down that road to the little schoolhouse that was our destination. She had walked in the drifted snow of winter and in the bright, flowering mornings of May. As we drove into the schoolyard, she would say with that wonderful gaiety she never lost, "This is the only place in the world where your mother was a second baseman!" There it would be still, the primitive baseball diamond where she played at recess with the Glass and the Grieshaber and the Shane and the Reinheimer kids.

My father would loosen the check rein on Alice and give her a nose bag of oats, my brother would go to the pump and rattle vigorously away at it until the water, cold from the deep pipe and tasting of the sweet limestone through which it ran, came splashing into his bucket. My sisters would spread out the clean horse blanket and help my mother unpack our lunch. We always had a jug with lemon juice and sugar and would fill it with the icy water, so that we had lemonade drawn, as it were, from under the field where my mother had played baseball with the farm boys many years before. Under the white oak trees, on the grass so green and heavy it seemed to have grown a measurable height just while we sat there, we ate the cold chicken with crisp homemade dill pickles (there was wild dill growing along the edge of the field) and fresh-baked bread.

Rested, we would pack up and drive on to the country cemetery where my father's mother was buried. This was a tiny place where all the graves were of neighbors with whom my father's family had exchanged work when someone was ill. On all sides were cornfields and pastures, and when we arrived, cattle would come up to the fence and stare across, their brown eyes (they were always Jerseys and Guernseys) as deep as the wells and springs we had seen that day, as liquid and as alive. They stood there quietly and with the stolid poise of those who had come to pay their own friendly respects to the dead.

"This is nice," my mother said on the Memorial Day when I was eight, "this is nice." Sitting on the path, holding her large plumed and feathered hat on her lap, she watched the cemetery busy with people mowing and cutting and trimming.

Although my brother, older, larger, and stronger, usually pushed the old lawn mower, I would be allowed to do it on such Memorial Days as I had the courage to walk over the graves. It always gave me a ghostly feeling to wander crookedly over the one mound we had come to visit. It felt as if the ground was unsteady beneath me, pitching and tossing slightly, and I would hang on to the handle of the mower for fear of being upset and pulled down below the grass.

The general mood, however, was bright and lively. We would put out the tame and wild flowers we had brought, set one of the wild rosebushes dug up along the road, and watch others moving about filling vases and calling warmly to each other. There would always be friends who came over to recall the cherished past. Some had known my grandmother and would say enthusiastically, "My, she certainly would have liked the lilacs."

By now it would be late afternoon, the grave would be neat and gay, and the fresh smell of cut grass, flowers, plowed field, pasture, and evergreen would be heavy in the air. So again we would load the wagon and settle down wearily in the rustling straw.

When you start an auto and turn home, it is still the same mechanical process, but a horse is a revived and eager animal when you head it down a fine country road toward its barn. It steps out with liveliness, you can feel its anticipation carried up through the reins in your hand, and I could feel it even in the ends which I would clutch as Alice trotted off toward town. The sand would rise on the iron rim of the wheel and fall away with a tiny whispering sound. The wagon itself seemed to feel Alice's cheerfulness and bounced along with a gayer motion. The straw gleamed more golden as the sun's light thickened in the west.

The children would grow sleepy with the jogging of the horse and the rocking of the wagon. My younger sister would curl up with her doll and doze off, while my older sister talked dresses with Mother. My brother would argue the glories and disasters of the local baseball team, called the Bunnies, which leapt around the diamond with rabbits on their shirts. As we drove into the street by our house and tied Alice to the hitching post, Father would slap her on the rump and say, "That's what she's needed, a real workout on the road." Alice would toss her head in a tired acknowledgment that the remark was probably true.

My brother had to go on to the barn to help with the horses, but I was small enough to be sent right to bed after a sandwich and a glass of milk. The whole long day had been a family affair, and I hated to leave the human closeness, which was so much warmer than on an ordinary day. The taste of water from the spring, the feel of cold water from the schoolhouse pump, the colorful brightness of tiny American flags, the smell of the sun hot on thorny rosebushes, the cud-grinding cows peering over the fence with animal curiosity, the farm families we met already tanned with working in the fields—these memories were jammed into my head as I trudged off to sleep.

Our Memorial Day was observed, not to remind the living of the dead, but to assure the dead that life still went on, in all its luck and wonder, over the face of the remembering earth.

That Fabulous Old Fourth of July

We won the American Revolution, but we lost the Fourth of July.

Of course, I believe in the "Safe and Sane Fourth" and am grateful that my children are growing up without losing fingers to badly made firecrackers or eyes to misfiring Roman candles. But in my heart, I mourn that wonderful, mad, violent day. For a little while, we shared a little of the risk that the old Continental troops had taken. Handling firecrackers, setting off rockets, blasting tin cans into the air — somehow we were close to that dangerous original event.

It seemed right to take that risk. After all, there was little safe about the life of those small armies straggling up and down the dark eastern wilderness. And there was little really sane about those divided and weak colonies opposing one of the great powers of Europe. And yet, like them, we survived, we triumphed.

We killed no enemy (unless you counted the extra lives that outraged cats left behind as they flew over fences), but we did start our short day, as those firm farmers at Concord Bridge had started their long war, with an explosion of powder.

When I was a boy in an Iowa town, every neighborhood kid of twelve sneaked off at dawn to the blacksmith shops. There the blacksmith, powerful in the pride of his brawny arms and his split-leather apron, and already blackened around his face, would put a big charge of powder on an anvil. Then he would insert a fuse and put another anvil on top of that. When ignited, the powder blew up with a tremendous roar and crash of iron, blasting indignant citizens from their beds, sending dogs howling under cellars and bushes, terrifying horses so that they stamped their shod feet and whinnied from their barns.

After the anvils, we scattered to burn up in a few hours the fireworks we had bought with our painfully earned money, acquired by mowing lawns, selling newspapers, bottles, junk. All over town the debauch of our savings went on, a noise like the skirmishing of muskets, such sounds as our children do not know. What else booms like a giant firecracker lit and wildly thrown down a sewer, its long underground roar echoing through the hollow pipes? You could put your ear to the manhole cover and feel the vibration. There were the red "sons-o'-guns" which sputtered and crackled when rubbed over the sidewalk and would go tearing into your legs if you dropped a rock on them. And there would be the delicate splatter of tiny "ladyfingers" firing. We would light whole strings and throw them into the air, to catch in trees and carry on a private spitting war at each other.

Sometimes the bigger boys would turn up with a crude cannon made from iron pipe plugged at one end. We would lie on the slopes above those lawn-artillery men, dreading (and yet secretly hoping) that the whole infernal machine would blow up, as it often did, and those heroes would be carried home howling. The streetcars were a vivid help, too. We would put rows of torpedoes along the track and watch them shatter sideways with a ruddy flare. The progress of a motorman across town was one long explosion. I have wondered since at how patiently they endured our follies.

Not only are those noises gone, but so are the smells — above all the dense, brown odor of punk smoldering. A stick of punk would give just enough live coal to ignite firecracker fuses. Nothing else in the world had that damp, persistent smell; mingled with burning powder, it made the air itself seem scorched. My grandfather always said that it rained so much during Civil War battles because the gunpowder brought it out of the clouds. I would stand there sniffing, to see if our little effort might not produce at least a shower.

It was a terrible day for animals. Cats and dogs hid as deep under barns and houses as they could get and only came out late at night, trembling and whining. But horses had to be out in that inferno. My father always drove a horse and buggy home from work, tying up that poor animal at the curb. I would be sent out to put a nose bag of oats on it, and in my hands today I can feel the tall, strong creature shaking as fire-crackers went off and hear its iron shoes scratching on the brick paving.

The biggest event was always the parade and in that parade the most important group for us was the Civil War veterans' group, for my grandfather was among them. They had all been in the Union army. My grandfather had been a cavalryman and considered it debasing to march like infantry. He was a big, gentle man with a tremendous white beard, which he would trim before the mirror as he prepared for the parade.

It was hard for me to think of that quiet man, snipping at a few straggling whiskers, as a desperate young soldier. Yet when he had put on his blue uniform and braced himself for the march that he would not admit was exhausting, there would be in his effort to stand perfectly erect, in spite of his farmer's stoop, such a fierce determination that I could suddenly imagine the whole bloody and frantic moments of a young trooper's life. His jaw would set as I never saw it through the rest of the year, and he would step out with a grim look on his face that scared me. He had earned that stoop, as he had earned that uniform, the hard, hard way: by hanging on to a hand plow over his fields.

I remember still the Fourth of July when Grandfather had a savage moral dilemma — the summer that the family felt he was not strong enough to walk the distance of the parade. He shouted that it was bad enough for a cavalryman to walk like a foot soldier, but by the eternal, it was a disgrace to ride in a stinking automobile. His daughter, my mother, argued that he had to do it, "to be with the boys." Muttering in his beard, his face a furious red under the white hair, he gave in, his worst defeat of the war, and rode in an open horseless carriage with a few other casualties of age, sitting there grim and erect and ashamed. Somehow, seeing that venerable pride, I confused him with the soldiers who had fought that eighteenth-century war whose Declaration of Independence we were celebrating, thus casually adding a hundred years to the seventy he already had.

Along with the risk to hands and eyes, there was one more menace on the Fourth of July—the public oration. This was always delivered from the bandstand in the middle of the block-square park in the center of town. It was expected to produce suffering as cruel as the war itself, with its tortuous length and its rhetoric exploding like shrapnel, and it usually did.

The audience stood there sweltering in the sun, unflinching in the face of volley after volley of murderous oratory. The speaker worked and sweated as hard as any infantryman marching through Georgia. He defended the Constitution fiercely, to an audience not precisely hostile to that noble document. There was always some pounded-home-with-the-fists praise of that sterling native stock that was the backbone of the country. This my grandfather took seriously indeed, although his family came from Europe and he spoke German before he learned English. Thanks were given to God for providing so few Indians to be chased from this fertile soil, and thanks were given to the Milwaukee Railroad for sending a brass band. Motherhood was so vigorously defended, I had the impression the glorious revolution had been fought so that women could bear children.

While this flowerpot of fancy language was blossoming out of the bandstand, there was always a handful of daring boys skulking on the fringes of the crowd, throwing lighted firecrackers at each other. The boldest would stand near a horse tied to a hitching post and smash a cane, red-white-and-blue, with a cap in one end which exploded with a sharp snap, causing the horse to rear and plunge. Small children would crouch over little mounds which, when the point was lit, would send out twisting brown snakes. Usually snakes and children were stepped on as the crowd shifted, and piercing shrieks would ascend to heaven along with the speech.

Finally the orator would conclude with the startling pronouncement that "universal prosperity is everywhere, even in Iowa," and our ordeal would end. Then we went off to another two hours of agony, that furious trial by food called the Fourth of July picnic. We usually drove to the banks of the Cedar River, where a collection of food was spread out as if a hard-riding, hungry regiment were expected any moment. All of it would be from the home farm; the fried chicken, the ham, the pickles (dill, sweet, watermelon), huge loaves of bread baked in the iron stove, butter churned that morning.

Best of all for the children was the ice cream, which was made right on the spot (and it had real cream in it, too). The can would be covered with chipped ice and salt, and we would all take turns at the handle, enthusiastically at first and then wearily; but the rule was, "One hundred strokes after it gets hard to turn." Finally the great moment came when the lid was knocked off and the dasher pulled out, all dripping with the best ice cream ever made and eaten by the same hands that milked the cow that gave the cream. But of course the cover would be replaced until after the other food had been eaten, and that was another ordeal to be endured. Anything less than painful overeating was considered disloyal.

Afterward, Grandfather always said he didn't need a nap, but he would be asleep before we had taken our long bamboo poles to the river and hung on our hooks the most formidable catfish bait to be had anywhere: chicken entrails that had been put in a glass jar and hung three days in the sun to "ripen." The stench of that bait joined with the other Fourth of July smells to enrich our noses and to linger on our hands. Then the loading of the wagon, and home.

Night brought its own glories and dangers. Sparklers would dazzle the dark with their sudden light, and pinwheels would hiss and whirr where they were nailed on trees. Some child was always burned by walking into a Roman candle. By night we had much more the feeling of the whole town celebrating, because we could not only hear the racket but also see the many colored lights in the sky. We would use a rainspout for launching skyrockets, and it would be a magnificent moment when we waited, in our miniature impatience, for the rocket to burst from the end of the spout and tear into the blackness with a trail of fire.

The day ended as the celebration of a time of danger and triumph should end: dirty, exhausted, blistered, and bandaged, we struggled off to bed. A battle, in which only one side fired, had been won. The country was safe for another year, and so were we.

There were two final night noises audible as I crept upstairs to bed. One was the last boom of distant nightworks going off in the sky (I could see their flash through the open window like signal lights calling me back into the struggle, but I could not go). The other was the steady voice of my grandfather saying, with tiredness and resolution equally strong, "We were camped that night, it was in '64, along the banks of the . . ." I never heard the name of that far stream, because, as I was mumbling that I couldn't go to sleep so soon, I fell asleep.

And now I will never know what river.

Where the World Seems Right and Good —
The Iowa State Fair

If all you saw of life was the Iowa State Fair on a brilliant August day when you could hear those incredible crops ripening out of the black dirt between the Missouri and Mississippi Rivers, you would believe that this was surely the best of all possible worlds.

You would have no sense of the destruction of life, only of its rich creativeness: no political disasters, no assassinations, no ideological competition, no wars, no corruption, no atom waiting in its dark secrecy to destroy us all with its exploding energy.

There is a lot of energy at the Fair in Des Moines, but it is all peaceful. The double giant Ferris wheel rotates, its swaying seats more frightening than a jet plane flying through a monsoon. Eighty thousand men, women, and children walk all day and much of the night across the fairgrounds. Ponies pick up their feet in a slashing trot as if the ground burned them. Hard rock music backgrounds the soft lowing of a Jersey cow in the cattle barn over her newborn calf the color of a wild deer. Screaming speeches are made all around the world urging violence; here there are plenty of voices, but they are calling for you to throw baseballs at kewpie dolls, to pitch nickels at a dish that won't hold them, to buy cotton candy, corndogs, a paring knife that performs every useful act save mixing a martini.

Above all, you would believe there was no hunger in the world, for what the Iowa State Fair celebrates is not only peace but food. This is one of the few places in the world where you see every condition of food. It walks by you on the hoof, Hereford, Angus, Charolais, Shorthorn steer, the meat under their hides produced by a beautifully balanced diet more complicated than a baby's formula. These thousand-pound beef animals look at you with their oval, liquid eyes, not knowing that in human terms they are round steak, rib roast, tenderloin, chuck, hamburger. Did I actually see them turn away in disgust as they walked past the sizzling hamburger stand?

The Fair has always specialized in show ring competition for swine and cattle, but in recent years this has been extended to the final moment of truth, the slaughtered and dressed carcass. Often the animal which won on the hoof will not actually be as good a meat specimen as one graded lower on its "figure." Probably the most important single event at the Fair is also the quietest and most hidden: the judging of the carcass by experts in long white coats in a refrigerated room. The months of elaborate feeding, of care to prevent injuries or bruises, all have their meaning when the loin-eye is measured and the balance between fat and lean is revealed. At the 1974 Fair, Roy B. Keppy's crossbred hog placed second in the live competition but first in the pork carcass show. It yielded a chop which measured 6.36 square inches, one of the largest in the history of the Fair. A little more than an inch of fat covered the rib (loin-eye) area, the tenderest part of the whole animal.

If you saw close-up the boys and girls of 4-H, you would also believe that this world was lived in by the best of all possible people. These are not the drugged youth of the newspapers. They are intelligent and sturdy youngsters who have carried into the present years the old-fashioned and sturdy ideas: the 4-H concept means thinking Head, feeling Heart, skilled Hand, and strong Health. They walk with the ease of the physically active and the confidence of people who have done serious and useful projects. They understand animals, machines, fibers. Nor are they the "hicks" of rural legend. Newspapers, radio, television have brought the world into their home; before their eyes they see what is happening not only in the nearest city but in a country five thousand miles away. Nor are they dull—often a 4-H boy and girl will work together washing down their steers, shampooing the tails, polishing the hooves, and then go off to spend the evening dancing or at a rock concert.

One of the great sights in 4-H at the Fair is the weeping face of a bright, attractive farm girl whose steer has just won a championship. She has raised the animal herself, if not from birth then from a few months old. She has kept a daily record of how much she fed it each day, of how many pounds of feed it took to make how many pounds of gain (a corn-fed beef steer's daily growth is frightening and fattening). She has washed and brushed and combed it, taught it to be led with a halter, to stand still on order. The final moment of truth comes when she leads it into the show ring and the judge examines it with a hard and expert eye for flaws and for excellence, for depth of brisket between the front legs, for curve of rump and sense of fat under the skin. If a blue ribbon is awarded, tears of joy mark the cheeks of the 4-H girl, after her months of loving care and the tension of competing. Then the auction, for which she receives much more per pound than the average because she has the champion, with tears of sadness because the creature that had become a pet at home is led off to be slaughtered. The Head, Heart, Hand, and Health of that devoted female person went into the profitable health of that sexless steer.

One of the dramatic examples of energy at the Fair is in the tractor, draft team, and pony pulls in which the machine and the animals rear up as they try to pull a weighted sledge. The golden feel of new oat straw, the fleece of Oxford Down or Shropshire lambs, the green surface of a John Deere eight-row corn picker, smooth as skin and tough as steel, the sweet stickiness of cotton candy.

"Ear" has almost too much to take in: the hog-calling contest with its shrill shrieks, the husband-calling contest combining seduction with threats, the whinnying of Tennessee walking horses, the lowing of cattle bored with standing in the show ring, the male-chauvinist crowing of roosters at the poultry barn, loudest at daybreak (the champion crowed 104 times in half an hour), the merry-go-round playing its old sentimental tunes, the roar of racing cars, the barkers praising the promised beauty to be revealed at the girlie show, the old fiddlers' contest vibrating the air with "Buffalo Gal," "Texas Star," and "Tennessee Waltz," the clang of horseshoes against each other and against the stake.

"Tongue" learns the taste of hickory-smoked ham, the richness of butter on popcorn with beer, the tang of rhubarb pie, the sour elegance of buttermilk served ice cold, the total smack of hamburger with onion, pickle, mustard, and horseradish, many-flavored ice cream, chicken fried in sight of their live cousins in the poultry barn, barbecued pork ribs spitting their fat into the fire as fattened hogs waddle by on their way to be judged.

"Nose" has an exhausting time at the Fair. It smells the many odors rising from the grills of men competing in the Iowa Cookout King contest, grilling turkey, lamb, beef, pork, chicken, ham with backyard recipes which excite the appetite; the delicate scents of flowers in the horticulture competition; the smells of homemade foods; the crisp smell of hay. People drive hundreds of miles in air-conditioned cars that filter out smells in order to walk through the heavy and hot late-summer air across the manure-reeking atmosphere of the hog, cattle, horse, and sheep barns to sniff again the animal odors of their childhood.

You can watch the judging of home-baked bread or listen to the latest rock group. You can watch free every day the teenage talent search or pay money to hear the same nationally known acts you can watch free on television. The 4-H sewing contest in which contenders wear the clothes they made was startled in 1974 to have a boy enter himself and his navy-blue knit slacks and jacket with white trim. He grew up on a hog farm but wanted to design clothes. A girl won.

The Iowa State Fair is a great annual ceremony of the sane. Young girls still stand all night behind dairy cows with pitchforks to keep the freshly washed animals from getting dirty before being shown in the morning. Boys milk cows at 10 P.M., 2 A.M., and 3 A.M. to be sure their udders are "balanced" when judges look at them. This is hardly the kind of teenager about whom we hear most often. A six-year-old boy wins the rooster crowing contest. There is Indian Wrestling (arm-hand wrestling) with a white and a black sweating in immobile silence; the judge is John Buffalo, an Indian from the settlement near Tama.

Year after year this rich and practical ritual of life is repeated. Animals whose ancestors competed many Fairs ago come back. So do people, returning by plane and automobile to the grounds their grandparents visited by train and buggy. Three-hundred-and-fifty-horsepower internal-combustion engines have replaced the one-horse hitch and the two-horse team, but the essential objects of life are the same: the dented ear of corn, the rounded rib of steer and pig, that nourishment of the human race which is the prime purpose of this plowing and harvesting State of Iowa.

To some, the Fair seems corny. To others, the world still needs to catch up to the human and animal decency which each year dignifies a corner of this corrupt world. A few hundred acres of human skill and animal beauty in Des Moines, Iowa, prove to the space capsule of earth how to live.

Our Dangerous Thanksgiving

As our grandfather lifted his long carving knife to cut the first slice of meat, we could see hanging on the wall behind him the saber he had carried as a cavalryman in the Civil War. It was the right ornament for our Thanksgiving, which was not only a holiday but something of a battle in which the participants groaned as well as the loaded table.

Nostalgic paintings of early-twentieth-century families looking over the endless food always show relaxed and smiling faces. Of course, we were cheerful, too, for in that less complicated time it was easily assumed that, if a man worked seven fourteen-hour days a week (with a little time between chores on Sunday for prayer), he would be rewarded with a decent meal in November.

In my childhood Thanksgiving, however, there was not only obvious joy but also a certain desperate struggle. The Lord had challenged us with all those huge and heavy dishes. We could not let Him down. We fought the good fight with knife, fork, and raw courage. In the end, we proved that we had in us not only dutiful thanks but the power of survival as well.

Watching Grandfather delicately sever a turkey neck to go into giblet gravy, it was hard to think of that gentle man swinging his curved saber at a human throat. When asked about the Sioux Indians he had fought, he would always say, "They were a noisy outfit. You never heard such yelling." Then, lifting his hands as if they again held the supple leather reins, not knife and carving fork, he would add with a grin, "But I did some pretty good howling myself, boy."

Like a blessing at the start of a hard campaign, grace was said at length. Obviously, the Almighty had to listen to a lot of invocations at that same moment, and if ours wasn't long and loud enough it might not be heard. This was a very tense time, that waiting for the first clash of our weapons for eating. My uncle George, who came farthest to join us, having gone to Idaho as a young man, would clench and unclench his hands in his lap, knocking his fists against each other like a fighter before a bout.

Grandfather had the right to bless that meal, for everything in it save coffee, sugar, and cranberries he had raised himself. The hands that carved the bird had also set the eggs in the nest, raised the grain which it was fed, built the rack where it roosted and the pen where it was fattened, and had finally shoved its head between two bent nails on the chopping block and killed it with one blow of the hatchet while his left hand held the kicking legs.

Unlike in wartime, what was slaughtered was not the enemy but an old friend, raised from a chick, which often followed Grandfather around the yard clucking at him and sometimes gobbling down from a tree. Once he forgot to bury the bloody head, and when the cousins found it they screamed louder than the bird dragged to its doom. Hours later at the kitchen their tears still fell, adding a salty tang to the cake dough they were stirring.

Grandfather wonderfully combined in his uttering of the "Amen" at the end of his prayer the restraint of a final word to God and the excitement of a cavalry command. The adults at the big table, the adolescents at the medium table, and the little kids at the tiny one, wearied with giving thanks by words, now proved their gratitude by competing for food. The faint of heart retired from combat after only two or three servings, but the bravest kept on slashing with their knives and spearing with their forks and dipping with their spoons.

As at any athletic competition, there were cries and cheers. "Look at George, that's his fifth slice." "Tom, you've got to share that gravy with sixteen other people." "Tillie, you can't just eat your own gooseberry jam. Try that quince and apple preserve Gertrude brought." Every Thanksgiving one remark was always shouted at me, "Paulie, you can't stuff anything to eat in your pocket." But I did, with total lack of character and a thief's skill.

There were accusing eyes on us all the time. Grandfather had a coon hound accustomed to going up trees with low branches. He would jump into an apple tree outside the kitchen window and stare at us all through the meal, not barking, but making deep, rumbling noises in his throat as the smells of meat and bones tormented his blunt nose. Turkeys clung to branches just high enough to allow them to peer at the hideous carcass of their late friend. On the table was applesauce from that tree, and a plate of apples waited on the sideboard to be the last edible item on the menu. (It was generally considered that Aunt Rose's molasses cookies, served at the same time, were not edible.)

Beyond the yard was the field from which the dried sweet corn, now creamed, had come and the pumpkins that had rolled golden down the rows and were now dark brown in pies. Next to it was the garden from which the yellow and green beans had been harvested (I put in hours hoeing and weeding them on summer visits, so that I, too, earned my appetite) and the cabbage and squash now buried in a barrel of sand. It was all close at hand, all shaped and tendered by hand. I felt Aunt Gertrude's calluses on her fingers when she welcomed me each Thanksgiving morning—what woman now has skin rough from raising the food she is serving you?

There was always the bitterest conflict of the day between my uncles George and Charlie, to see who remained eating and upright to the last. After everyone had lapsed into a paralysis of arm and stomach, we would take sides: "Attaboy, George, one more piece of roast and you've got him beat." But then Charlie would rear back and lunge at a thigh joint of duck and be back in the struggle. The final test was to prove that you had eaten something from every dish on the table. That was tough, because it was not a matter of many different varieties of food but of many variations within each type. This was not merely a bowl of sweet or dill pickles—there were spiced beets, pickled watermelon rind, cauliflower, and cherries, even prunes to which strange things had been done with vinegar and herbs.

There was no fruit of the region not represented in jam or jelly, all gathered by the cousins and cooked by Aunt Gertrude.

There was cottage cheese from the bags hanging in the dark cave of an earth basement, cabbage in the form of fresh coleslaw and as sauerkraut. Hickory-nut cake was the noblest, because it meant the greatest labor. There were also angel food, upside-down cake, butternut (where have all the trees of this succulent, smooth nut gone?), and black walnut, so oily and rich. The pies were apple, mince, butterscotch, peach, cherry. Every one of these was a personal menace to George and Charlie, who were tempted to finish with a little dish of spiced Whitney crab apple but under our observing eyes, out of deference to Gertrude's cooking, out of honor to the Lord who had provided, and out of stubborn determination to do better than last Thanksgiving, resolutely worked their way through at least a sample of everything.

Wounded in soul and gut, the uncles called it a draw, as they did every year, and staggered off to sleep the sleep of heroes on couches. Hearing the stir of people rising from table, the cats outside began to mew pathetically, the dogs barked in anticipation, the children were threatened into clearing dishes from the tables, aunts drew water from the reservoir alongside the fire in the kitchen range ("Don't let those dishes wait, they'll never get washed in time for supper," was Aunt Tillie's unbelievable remark), and the other men went outside to look at the fallow fields, from which all our nourishment had come, and to walk off the edges of the meal, to let the mince pie with homemade ice cream (the cows who gave the milk watched us over the fence) shake down on the pickled green tomatoes.

The last survivor was my grandmother, asleep on the sofa with the freshly ironed handkerchief over her face softly rising and falling, as her breathing, deep from the work of the day, proved that the small heart inside was giving thanks that it was also tough and could endure.

Christmas Eve and My Mother's Hands

The sharpest memory of our old-fashioned Christmas Eve is my mother's hand making sure I was settled in bed. Although her fingers moved gently in the dark of that excited night, they scratched my face with their roughness.

Mother had been sewing for months, making useful and sturdy garments for the children, two boys and two girls. With all the baking, shopping, and decorating she had to do, it was natural for her to fall behind in the last days before Christmas. That meant sewing not only late at night but also rapidly. Since much of it was done by hand, she would stab her fingers with the needle, making them a little torn and rough. Some years, the first Christmas red I saw would be a drop of blood at the tip of Mother's finger.

All evening I would fight sleep, as if it were a dark angel come to take me out of that bright world where real wax candles burned and wavered dangerously on the tree. The house would be almost loud with the tantalizing smells of things baking, boiling, frying, bubbling on the stove. The sweet of maple sugar blended with the sour of vinegar in a single odor, like a child's gay-sad cry.

If I went to sleep, wasn't there a good chance that I might wake up to find that the whole glittering night had been imagined, and it would just be an ordinary winter day, with the drifted sidewalks to shovel? So I became an active nuisance, stealing cookies, pestering my sisters (one older, one younger) at their sewing, and hovering at the edge of Mother's bustling activity.

All evening Mother would run—literally, for there was no time, in those last few hours, to walk—from sewing machine to kitchen, whirring at the machine and then stirring at the stove. Between these mechanisms, she would do small bits of hand sewing, and these were the loveliest moments of all. In the sewing drawer of her rocking chair, along with all the buttons and other sewing materials, were colorful pincushions shaped like green frogs and yellow pumpkins. One pincushion was a large strawberry, from which hung, by a green string, a little strawberry with tiny green leaves. The smaller berry was filled with powdered emery, and Mother would plunge a needle rapidly in it, to clean and sharpen the point.

Always in motion, she would rock steadily while doing the fine stitches on my sister's skirt or an embroidered blouse for a cousin or a coat for me. Swiftly, swiftly the point of the needle would leap, as quick and sharp as the points of light in her eyes, and then suddenly it would make a wrong jump and stab a finger. Mother would call, "Darn! Even if I do say it." Her cry would not be in pain but in distress at the pace of her work being slowed just when she was hurrying her fastest.

The break would be a bad one for me, too, since she usually saw me sitting there on the floor, yawning, and said, "Up to bed, now, or you won't have time to come down in the morning." I would drag myself grimly off and even in bed would force myself to stay awake, guessing what the downstairs noises meant, for once again the sewing machine would start its unsteady rush. It was an old foot-treadle type, which Mother could speed up or slow down by the pressure of her nimble feet.

Sometimes the rush of sewing would stop, and I could hear Mother's urgent step running to put another finished present under the tree or take from the oven that wonderful bread she made only at Christmas, with raisins, quince, black walnut, and hickory nuts inside and a glaze of cinnamon and brown sugar on the outside. Or the steps would be only a few, and then I would hear the solid-oak rocking of the little chair as she sewed the fine and durable stitches. Next morning, I would see in my new shirt the rhythmic pattern of that rocking worked out by her steady needle and her punished fingers and her child-loving heart.

Then would come the time when her steps climbed up to my bedroom, and in the back cold of the unheated room I waited for the old, familiar sound — the creak as her foot hit the fifth tread from the top, which always bent and groaned a little. Then her rush across the floor and her warm hand scratching back and forth over my forehead. That rough hand was more reassuring than a smooth one, for it meant that the good Christmas activity had been going on long enough to break the skin. That hand was proper part of the season, having made its own tiny blood sacrifice to the holiday.

Lulled by that rough and patient touch, I would sleep, impatient for the morning and its gifts of love and work.

No matter how late she had gone to bed, Mother was always up before the rest of us. Waking to the red sun burning like a great candle behind the frost trees on the window, I would creep farther down under the blankets for an instinctive instant. But then, hearing Mother's quick spoon beating the buckwheat batter for our breakfast pancakes, knocking against the yellow bowl with a rhythmic repetition of all those hard "b" sounds, I would know that the most beautiful morning of the year had begun. As most of our days began, and ended, with Mother's cheerful and industrious noise, it seemed only right that Christmas should begin that way.

By the time my feet hit the icy floor and reached the stairway, my brother and sisters would be floating through space from the top step to the bottom, in what seemed, from above, one long glide. Below, we would face the two glowing wonders of Christmas: the tree, all its many-colored candles lighted, the tiny flames leaping upward to the homemade star gleaming with its candy-bar and chewing-tobacco tinfoil; and our mother, standing in the kitchen doorway, holding the yellow bowl and stirring the dark batter, her face glowing with the heat of cooking and with her excitement at our excitement.

In the kitchen, our father would already be attacking the first batch of pancakes before going off to work at six o'clock, as he did every morning of the year. Under the tree would drift a white swirl of packages, most of them made right there in the next room. We were a poor family. Mother and Father worked long, hard, twelve-hour days. Christmas was always honored by their practical skills, their quiet belief in labor, and their devotion to us.

Were children ever so lucky?

An Old-Fashioned Christmas

Every Christmas should begin with the sound of bells, and when I was a child mine always did. But they were sleigh bells, not church bells, for we lived in a part of Cedar Rapids where there were no churches. My bells were on my father's team of horses and rang as he drove up to our hitching post with the bobsled that would take us to celebrate Christmas on the family farm, ten miles out in the country. My father would bring the team down 5th Avenue at a smart trot, flicking his whip over the horses' rumps and making the bells double their light, thin jangling over the snow, whose radiance threw back a brilliance like the sound of bells.

There are no such departures any more: the whole family piling into the bobsled that had a foot of golden oat straw to lie in and heavy buffalo robes to lie under, the horses stamping the soft snow, and at every motion of their hoofs the bells jingling, jingling. My father sat there with the reins firmly held, wearing his long horsehide coat and mittens, the deep chestnut color still glowing. It always troubled me as a boy of eight that the horses had so indifferent a view of their late friend appearing as a warm overcoat on the back of the man who put the iron bit in their mouths.

There are no streets like those any more: the snow sensibly left on the road for the sake of sleighs and easy travel. We would hop down and ride the runners; and along the streets we met other horses, so that we moved from one set of bells to another, from the tiny tinkle of the individual bells on the shafts to the silvery, leaping sound of the long strands hung over the harness. There would be an occasional brass-mounted automobile laboring on its narrow tires and as often as not pulled up the slippery hills by a horse, and we would pass it with a triumphant shout, for it was an awkward nuisance, obviously not here to stay.

The country road ran through a landscape of little hills and shallow valleys and heavy groves of timber, including one of great towering black walnut trees which were all cut down a year later to be made into gunstocks for World War I. The great moment was when we left the road and turned up the long lane on the farm. It ran through fields where watermelons were always planted in the summer because of the fine sandy soil, and I could go out and break one open to see its Christmas colors of green skin and red insides.

Nearing the low house on the hill, with oaks on one side and apple trees on the other, my father would stand up, flourish his whip, and bring the bobsled right up to the door with a burst of speed.

There are no such arrivals any more: the harness bells ringing and clashing like faraway steeples, the horses whinnying at the horses in the barn and receiving a great, trumpeting whinny in reply, the dogs leaping into the bobsled and burrowing under the buffalo robes, a squawking from the hen house, a yelling of "Whoa, whoa," at the excited horses, boy and girl cousins howling around the bobsled, and the descent into the snow with the Christmas basket carried by my mother.

While my mother and sisters went into the house, the team was unhitched and taken to the barn, to be covered with blankets and given a little grain. That winter odor of barn is a wonderfully complex one, rich and warm and utterly unlike the smell of the same barn in summer: the body heat of animals, many weighing a thousand pounds and more; pigs in one corner making their dark, brown-sounding grunts; milk cattle still nuzzling the manger for wisps of hay; horses eyeing the newcomers and rolling their deep, oval eyes white; oats, hay, and straw tangy still with the live August sunlight; the manure steaming; the sharp odor of neat's-foot oil; the molasses-sweet odor of ensilage in the silo, where the fodder was almost fermenting. It is a smell from strong and living things, and my father always said it was the secret of health, that it scoured out a man's lungs; and he would stand there, breathing deeply, one hand on a horse's rump, watching the steam come out from under the blankets as the team cooled down from their rapid trot up the lane. It gave him a better appetite, he argued, than plain fresh air, which was thin and had no body to it.

A barn with cattle and horses is the place to begin Christmas; after all, that's where the original event happened, and that same smell was the first air that the Christ child breathed.

By the time we reached the house, my mother and sisters were wearing aprons and were busy in the kitchen, as red-faced as the women who had been there all morning. The kitchen was the biggest room in the house, and all family life save sleeping went on there. My uncle even had a couch along one wall where he napped and where the children lay when they were ill. The kitchen range was a tremendous black and gleaming Smoke Eater, with pans bubbling over the holes above the firebox and a reservoir of hot water at the side, lined with dull copper, from which my uncle would dip a basin of water and shave above the sink, turning his lathered face now and then to drop a remark into the women's talk, waving his straight-edged razor as if it were a threat to make them believe him. My job was to go to the woodpile out back and keep the fire burning. I split the chunks of oak and hickory, watching how cleanly the axe went through the tough wood.

It was a handmade Christmas. The tree came from down in the grove, and on it were many paper ornaments made by my cousins, as well as beautiful ones brought from the Black Forest. There were popcorn balls from corn planted on the sunny slope near the watermelons, paper horns with homemade candy, apples from the orchard. The gifts tended to be hand-knit socks, or wool ties, or fancy crocheted "yokes" for night-gowns, tatted collars for blouses, doilies with fancy flower patterns for tables, or tidies for chairs; once I received a brilliantly polished cow horn with a cavalryman crudely but bravely carved on it. And there would usually be a cornhusk doll, perhaps with a prune or a walnut for a face, and a gay dress from an old corset-cover scrap with its ribbons still bright. And there were real candles burning with real flames, every guest sniffing the air for the smell of scorching pine needles. No electrically lit tree has the warm and primitive presence of a tree with a crown of living fires over it, suggesting whatever true flame Joseph may have kindled on that original cold night.

There are no dinners like that any more: every item from the farm itself, with no deep freezer, no car for driving into town for packaged food. The pies had been baked the day before, pumpkin, apple, and mince. There was cottage cheese, with the dripping bags of curds still hanging from the cold cellar ceiling. The bread had been baked that morning, heating up the oven for the meat, and as my aunt hurried by I could smell in her apron that freshest of all odors with which the human nose is honored—bread straight from the oven. There would be a huge brown crock of beans with smoked pork from the hog butchered every November. We could see, beyond the crock, the broad black iron kettle in a corner of the barnyard, turned upside down, the innocent hogs stopping to scratch on it.

There would be every form of preserve: wild grape from the vines in the grove, crab-apple jelly, wild blackberry and tame raspberry, strawberry from the bed in the garden, sweet and sour pickles with dill from the rind of the same watermelon we had cooled in the tank at the milk house and eaten on a hot September afternoon.

Cut into the slope of the hill behind the house, with a little door of its own, was the vegetable cellar, from which came carrots, turnips, cabbages, potatoes, squash. Sometimes my scared cousins were sent there for punishment, to sit in darkness and meditate on their sins, but never on Christmas Day. For days after such an ordeal they could not endure biting into a carrot.

All the meat was from the home place, too. Most useful of all, the goose—the very one which had chased me the summer before, hissing and darting out its bill at the end of its curving neck like a feathered snake. Here was the universal bird of an older Christmas: its down was plucked, washed, and hung in bags in the barn to be put into pillows; its awkward body was roasted until the skin was crisp as a fine paper; and the grease from its carcass was melted down, a little camphor was added, and it was rubbed on the chests of coughing children. We ate, slept on, and wore that goose.

I was blessed as a child with a remote uncle from the nearest railroad town. Uncle Ben, who was admiringly referred to as a "railroad man," worked the run into Omaha. He had been to Chicago; "just often enough," his wife Minnie said with a sniff in her voice, "to ruin the fool, not often enough to teach him anything useful." Ben refused to eat fowl in any form, and as a Christmas token a little pork roast would be put in the oven just for him, always referred to by the hurrying ladies in the kitchen as "Ben's chunk." Ben would make frequent trips to the milk house, returning each time a little redder in the face, usually with one of the men at whom he had jerked his head. It was not many years before I came to associate Ben's remarkably fruity breath not only with the mince pie but with the jug I found sunk in the bottom of the cooling tank with a stone tied to its neck. He was a romantic figure to me for his constant travels and for that dignifying term "railroad man," so much more impressive than "farmer" or "lawyer." Yet now I see that he was a short man with a fine natural shyness, giving us knives and guns because he had no children of his own.

Of course, the trimmings were from the farm, too: the hickory-nut cake made with nuts gathered in the grove after the first frost and hulled by my cousins with yellowed hands: the black walnut cookies, sweeter than any taste; the fudge with butternuts crowding it. In the mornings we would be given a bowl of nuts to crack and pick out for the homemade ice cream.

And there was the orchard beyond the kitchen window, the Wealthy, the Russet, the Wolf with its giant-sized fruit, and an apple romantically called Northern Spy, as if it were a suspicious character out of the Civil War.

All families had their special Christmas food. Ours was called Dutch Bread, and a little round one was always baked for me in a Clabber Girl baking soda can, and my last act on Christmas Eve was to put it by the tree so that Santa Claus would find it and have a snack—after all, he'd come a long, cold way to our house. And every Christmas morning, he would have eaten it. My aunt made the same Dutch Bread, and we smeared over it the same butter she had been churning from their own Jersey milk (highest butterfat content) that same morning.

To eat in the same room where food is cooked—that is the way to thank the Lord for His abundance. The long table, with its different levels where additions had been made for the small fry, ran the length of the kitchen. The air was heavy with odors not only of food on plates but of the act of cooking itself, along with the metallic smell of heated iron from the hardworking Smoke Eater, and the whole stove offered us its yet uneaten prospects of more goose and untouched pies. To see the giblet gravy made and poured into a gravy boat, which had painted on its side winter scenes of boys sliding and deer bounding over snow, is the surest way to overeat its swimming richness.

The warning for Christmas dinner was always an order to go to the milk house for cream, where we skimmed from the cooling pans of fresh milk the cream that had the same golden color as the flanks of the Jersey cows that had given it. The last act before eating was grinding the coffee beans in the little mill, adding that exotic odor to the more native ones of goose and spiced pumpkin pie. Then all would sit at the table, and my uncle would say the grace, sometimes in German but later, for the benefit of us ignorant children, in English:

> Come, Lord Jesus, be our guest,
> Share this food that you have blessed.

There are no blessings like that any more: every scrap of food for which my uncle had asked the blessing was the result of his own hard work. What he took to the Lord for Him to make holy was the plain substance that an Iowa farm could produce in an average year with decent rainfall and proper plowing and manure.

The first act of dedication on such a Christmas was to the occasion that had begun it, thanks to the child of a pastoral couple who no doubt knew a good deal about rainfall and grass and the fattening of animals. The second act of dedication was to the ceremony of eating. My aunt kept a turmoil of food circulating, and to refuse any of it was somehow to violate the elevated nature of the day. We were there not only to celebrate a fortunate event for mankind but also to recognize that suffering was the natural lot of men — to consume the length and breadth of that meal was to suffer! But we all faced the ordeal with courage. Uncle Ben would let out his belt — a fancy western belt with steer heads and silver buckle — with a snap and a sigh. The women managed better by always getting up from the table and trotting to the kitchen sink or the Smoke Eater or outdoors for some item left in the cold. The men sat there grimly enduring the glory of their appetites.

After dinner, late in the afternoon, the women would make despairing gestures toward the dirty dishes and scoop up hot water from the reservoir at the side of the range. The men would go to the barn and look after the livestock. My older cousin would take his new .22 rifle and stalk out across the pasture with the remark, "I saw that fox just now looking for his Christmas goose." Or sleds would be dragged out, and we would slide in a long snake, feet hooked into the sled behind, down the hill and across the westward-sloping fields into the sunset. Bones would be thrown to dogs, suet tied in the oak trees for the juncos and winter-defying chickadees, saucers of skimmed milk set out for the cats daintily and disgustedly picking their padded feet through the snow, and crumbs scattered on a bird feeder where already the crimson cardinals would be dropping out of the sky like blood. Then back to the house for a final warming-up before leaving.

There was usually a song around the tree before we were all bundled up, many thanks given all around for gifts, the basket as loaded as when it came — even more so, for leftover food had been piled in it. My father and uncle would have brought up the team from the barn and hooked them into the double shafts of the bobsled, and we would all go out into the freezing air of early evening.

On the way to the door I would walk under a photograph of my grandfather, his cavalry saber hung over it. (I had once sneaked it down from the wall and in a flush of bravery had killed a mouse with it behind the corncrib.) With his long white beard he looked like one of the prophets in Hurlbut's illustrated *Story of the Bible*, and it was years before I discovered that as a young man he had not been off fighting the Philistines but rather the painted Sioux. It was hard to think of that gentle man, whose family had left Germany in protest over military service, swinging that deadly blade and yelling in a cavalry charge. But he had done just that, in some hard realization that sometimes the way to have peace and a quiet life on a modest farm was to go off and fight for them.

And now those bells again, as the horses, impatient from standing so long in the barn, stamped and shook their harness, my father holding them back with the soft clucking in his throat and a hard pull on the reins. The smell of wood smoke flavoring the air in our noses, the cousins shivering with cold, "Good-bye, good-bye," called out by everyone, and the bobsled would move off, creaking over the frost-brittle snow. All of us, my mother included, would dig down in the straw and pull the buffalo robes up to our chins. As the horses settled into a steady trot, the bells gently chiming in their rhythmical beat, we would fall half asleep, the hiss of the runners comforting us. As we looked up at the night sky through half-closed eyelids, the constant bounce and swerve of the runners would seem to shake the little stars as if they might fall into our laps. But that one great star in the east never wavered. Nothing could shake it from the sky as we drifted home on Christmas.

The Anti-Warrior: A Memoir
By Milt Felsen

Black Eagle Child:
The Facepaint Narratives
By Ray A. Young Bear

Fly in the Buttermilk:
The Life Story of Cecil Reed
By Cecil A. Reed with
Priscilla Donovan

In My Father's Study
By Ben Orlove

In Search of Susanna
By Suzanne L. Bunkers

Journey into Personhood
By Ruth Cameron Webb

Letters from Togo
By Susan Blake

A Lucky American Childhood
By Paul Engle

A Prairie Populist:
The Memoirs of Luna Kellie
Edited by Jane Taylor Nelsen

Taking Part: A Twentieth-
Century Life
By Robert Josephy

Tales of an American Hobo
By Charles Elmer Fox

Unfriendly Fire
By Peg Mullen

The Warsaw Sparks
By Gary Gildner